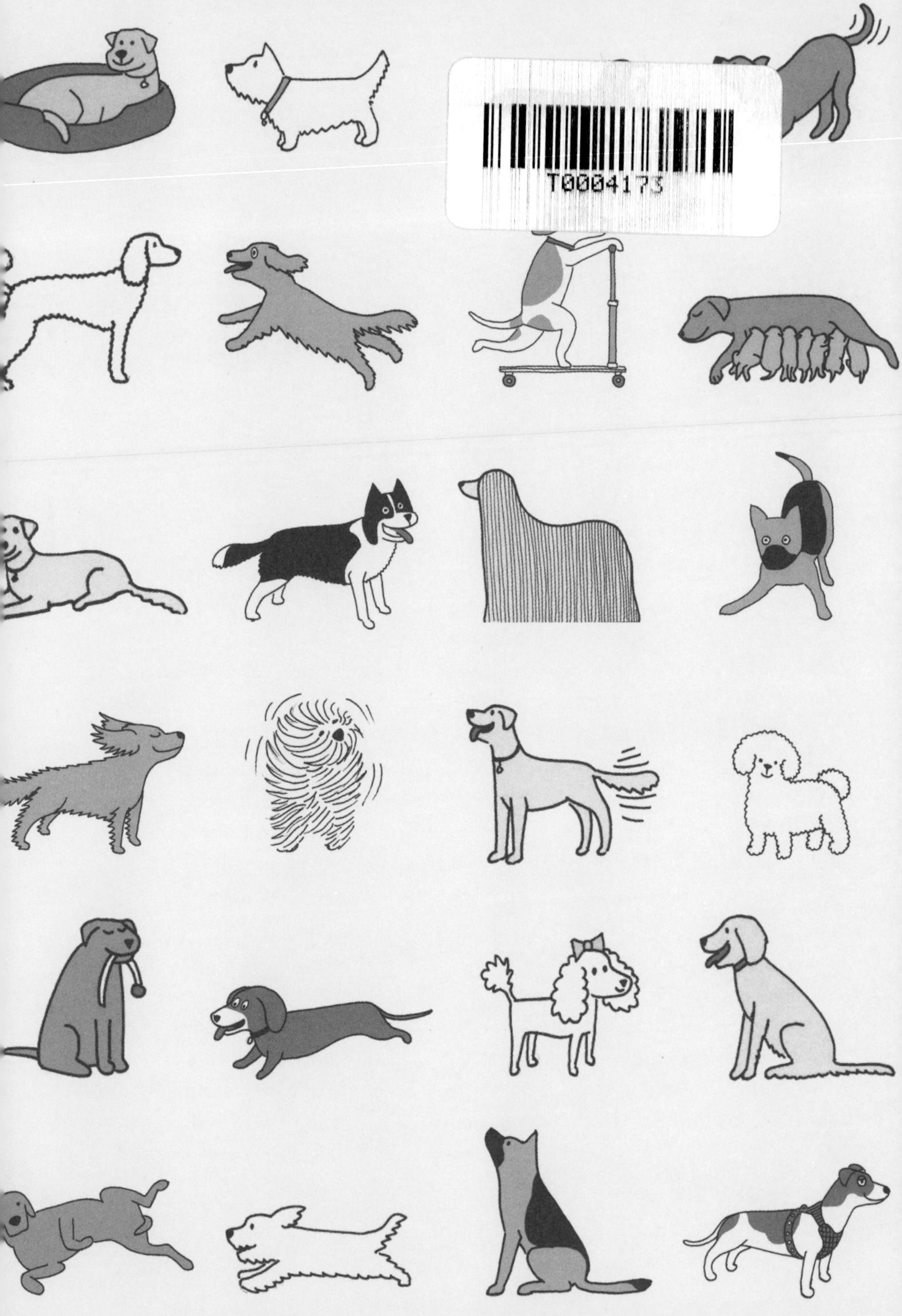

WHAT DOGS WANT

WHAT
DOGS
WANT

An illustrated guide for *truly*
understanding your dog

MAT WARD

BLOOMSBURY PUBLISHING
LONDON · OXFORD · NEW YORK · NEW DELHI · SYDNEY

To Trace, Finn, Lochie and the furry members of our family –
Pepper, Suki, Hemi and Limpet

ABOUT THIS BOOK

Everyone seems to have an opinion on dog behaviour and training. The amount of material in books and on the internet seems endless, and is often contradictory and confusing. How do you begin to separate the wheat from the chaff when digesting all this doggy information?

It's taken me 25 years of academic study and hands-on experience, with thousands of dogs and their guardians, to distil what's most important when caring for and training a dog. The information in this book represents the latest scientific understanding of our companion *Canis familiaris*, coupled with my real-world experience as a Clinical Animal Behaviourist. Whether you're thinking of adopting your first pup, or have a lifetime of experience with our four-legged friends, this book will help you understand your dog, train them effectively, and build a strong relationship with them. *It will allow you to focus on what's actually important as a dog guardian.*

After reading this book, and applying its advice, I'm confident your dog will be happier, and so will you!

Mat Ward BSc MVS CCAB
petbehavioursorted.com

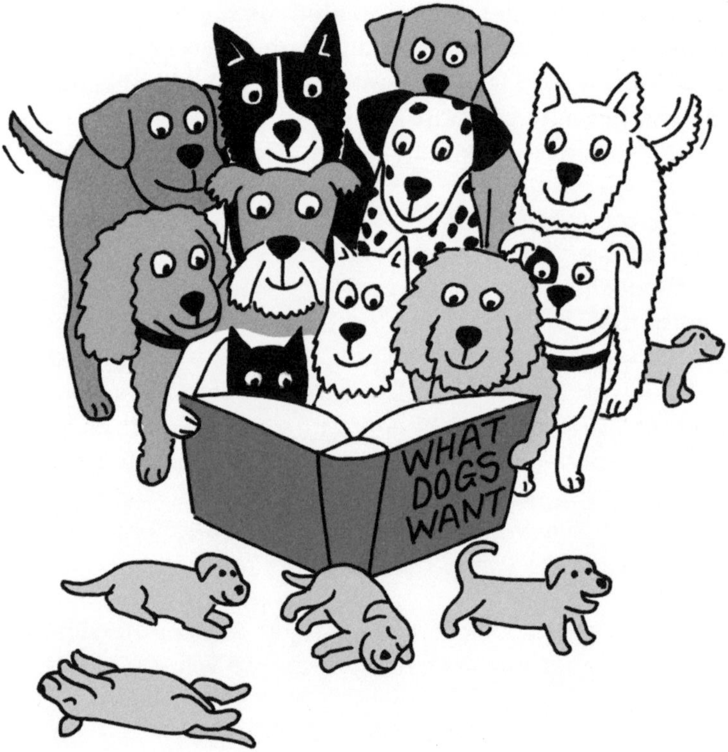
WHAT
DOGS
WANT

CONTENTS

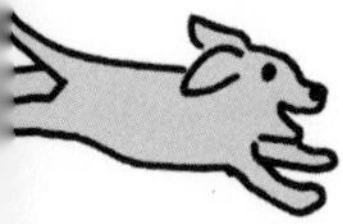

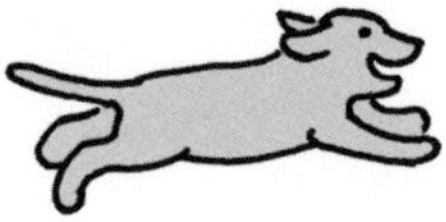

CHAPTER

1

IT'S A DOG'S LIFE

THE AMAZING NOSE

It's hard for us to imagine, but a dog's reality is more influenced by the way the world smells than the way it looks. To understand a dog, you need to understand their nose.

SUPER-SCENTERS

Did you know that dogs can identify smells as dilute as one part per trillion? That's one drop in twenty Olympic-sized swimming pools! In practical terms, your dog can tell which direction you walked off in by sniffing five of your footprints, and assessing how old the smell of each step is.

This amazing ability is a result of a number of special physical features. Dogs have a recess in their nose that traps 12% of inhaled air and is jam-packed with olfactory receptors. These receptors line a labyrinth of bony structures that maximise the available 'smelling' surface area. Dogs also have the mental processing power to make the most of this information – the area of their brain dealing with scents is at least three times larger than ours.

1

A window into the past

Smells help dogs to understand the world around them, not only in the present but also from the past. Think of it as smell CCTV!

Hmm, Patch has come by... he had a bath last night and has a new collar.

Peemails
Dogs are communicative creatures, but instead of reading emails, when out and about they read 'peemails'.

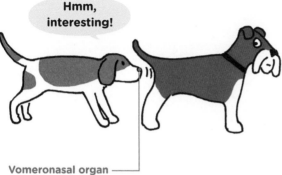

Hmm, interesting!

Vomeronasal organ
Dogs have a special organ near the front of their nose that is dedicated to sensing species-specific pheromones. These chemicals help communicate things such as fertility and other gender-related details.

2

Stereo smell

Each nostril samples air independently, which helps your dog to work out which direction a scent is coming from – in much the same way that we humans use our ears to tell where a sound is coming from.

Biodetection
Medical assistance dogs detect subtle changes in body chemicals in order to assist people with diabetes, Addison's disease and other disorders, by alerting them when they need medication. Dogs have also been taught to identify smells linked with cancer, which may help scientists develop machines to diagnose this disease from a breath sample.

3

Dogs with jobs

Dogs' brilliant noses and trainability make these four-legged friends the perfect candidates for jobs like search and rescue, truffle sniffing, explosives detection, and biodetection.

HOW DOGS SEE THE WORLD

Dogs see the world differently from us. They do well in the dark and have good peripheral vision, but don't see as sharply as we do, and can't differentiate some colours.

ARE DOGS COLOUR BLIND?

Dogs can see colour, but not as well as us. We have three types of colour receptor in our eyes (red, green and blue), but dogs have only two (yellow and blue). This means that while we see a full rainbow of colour, dogs see the range red, orange, yellow and green as one colour. Identifying a bright red ball in grass is a lot harder for a dog than it is for a human!

1

Night vision

Dogs see well at night. This is because of special features of their inner eye.

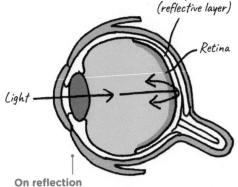

Tapetum (reflective layer)

Retina

Light

On reflection

Dogs have many 'rod' sensors in their retinas, which are very good at picking up light. Inside a dog's eye is a special reflective structure called the tapetum, which bounces light back to the retina, increasing a dog's ability to capture light at night.

I see you, Kitty!

2

Do I need glasses?

Dog vision is blurrier than ours. If dogs were able to take an eye test, they would achieve only 20/75. This means an object that appears clear to us at a distance of 75 feet, is clear to a dog only when they see it from a distance of 20 feet or closer.

Wide-angle lens

A dog's distance vision may not be as good as ours, but their field of view is much better. We can see 180 degrees; your average dog can see 240 degrees, depending on breed.

Built-in safety glasses

Chasing prey? Fighting? Shaking a toy? Don't worry, the nictitating membrane has a dog's eyes covered!

3

A third eyelid

Dogs have a third eyelid called the nictitating membrane, which helps clean and lubricate the eyes, produce antibodies to fight infection, and protect the eyes from damage.

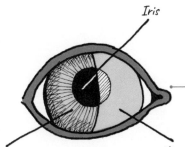

Iris

Cornea

Nictitating membrane

LISTEN UP!

There's nothing better than stroking the velvety ear of a dog while they snuggle into you, but those ears aren't just there for fun. They are serious pieces of equipment.

GOING ULTRASONIC

A dog's hearing is top notch, beating humans hands down in most respects. It is estimated to be four times as sensitive as ours – if you can hear the noise of a pin dropping on a wooden floor, your dog can hear it on a carpet...

Dogs are also able to hear sounds at much higher frequencies than we can – they can hear frequencies of 45kHz compared to our 20kHz max. Going ultrasonic is no problem at all for your average dog!

1

Furry satellite dishes

Dogs excel at identifying exactly where noises are coming from. Their independently moving outer-ears (pinnae) are able to rotate like a radar to locate the source of a sound.

Location, location, location!
A dog's brain makes instant calculations to work out where a sound came from, based on the tiny delay between the sound hitting one ear and then the other. When you see a dog tilting their head, it's thought to be their way of getting additional information for their speedy sums.

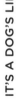

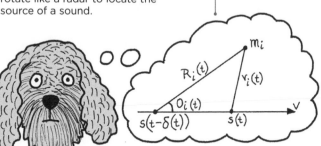

2

Designer ears

Over the centuries, as humans bred dogs for different purposes, the erect ear that is typical of the dog's ancestors evolved into many new shapes and sizes.

3

Deaf dogs

As dogs age, their hearing often gets worse. But dogs with certain colourings (such as white, piebald and merle) are more likely to be deaf from birth. This is because the genes that influence coat colour are also responsible for important parts of a dog's inner ear.

How do silent dog whistles work?
Silent dog whistles operate at a high pitch that dogs can hear, but we can't. This allows us to use the whistles for training dogs without annoying people nearby.

TASTE AND DIGESTION

Your dog's sense of taste is not nearly as well developed as their sense of smell... perhaps this is for the best given what they like to eat!

FAST FOOD

Dogs are programmed to eat quickly – in the wild the slowest eater might lose out altogether! Dogs have no need to chew their food to begin digestion. Instead they swallow big chunks, which their stomach acids then break down. From eating to pooing, the entire canine digestion process takes about eight hours. By comparison, a human's digestion takes a far more leisurely 24 hours.

1

Can dogs be vegetarian?

Surprisingly, yes! While cats are obligate carnivores (they have to eat meat to survive), dogs are omnivores – they can technically survive without meat. However, they have evolved to eat a meat-heavy diet, so take care if you're thinking of removing meat from your dog's food.

Veggies!

Valuable vet advice
If you are considering a vegetarian diet for your dog, do your research and speak to your vet before you begin.

How dogs drink
Dogs fold their tongue backwards to scoop up water and draw it upwards into their mouth.

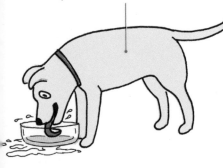

2

The taste of water

While water doesn't seem to be particularly flavoured for humans, dogs have special taste buds at the tip of their tongue that are highly sensitive to it. This may mean that water tastes delicious for your dog, causing them to drink plenty of it (a habit that happens to balance their meat-heavy diet).

Humans have better taste
Victory for humans! We win this sensory comparison with around 10,000 taste buds compared to a dog's 2,000.

3

Slobber safety issues

While having your dog lick you is usually fine for healthy people, avoid it if you are immunocompromised, or have any cuts or abrasions that would allow germs to get into your skin. Also try to avoid being licked on any of your own mucous membranes – your eyes, inside your nose, or inside your mouth – as these can provide routes of entry for nasty bacteria.

THE AGES OF DOG

When is a puppy ready to go to their new home? When does puberty hit? When is a dog an adult? How long will my dog live?

I'm not 2, I'm 21!

THE SEVEN-YEAR MYTH

Is one dog year really equivalent to seven human years? The simple answer is no. It may be a useful approximation for an adult dog, but it's way off for the early parts of a dog's life. For example, dogs hit puberty at around six months old – when was the last time you saw a three-year-old boy who needed a shave?!

A better way to think about it is to imagine that a dog has their 21st birthday when they turn two. After that, add five dog years for each human year that passes. For large breeds, it might be closer to six or seven dog years for every year, as larger dogs tend to have a shorter life expectancy (especially the giant breeds).

Phase of life	Age of dog (small breed)	Human equivalent	Specific development
Neonatal	0–2 weeks	0–6 months	Eyes and ears still closed. Eat, sleep, stay warm.
Transitional	2–3 weeks	6–9 months	Eyes and ears open. Teeth appear. First beginning to take in the world and learn to walk.
Socialisation	3 weeks	1 year	Beginning to eat solid food. Learning about their future social partners and environment. Broad experiences are critical. Ready to go to future home at 7–8 weeks. Vaccination programme finished by 10–12 weeks.
	6 weeks	3 years	
	9 weeks	5 years	
	12 weeks	6 years	
Juvenile	12 weeks	6 years	Honing basic life skills. Becoming more competent. Loving to chew. Play is life!
	4 months	9 years	
	5 months	11 years	
	6 months	13 years	
Adolescent	6 months	13 years	Puberty hits. Hormonal teenagers. Less inclined to listen to human parents. Increased emotional sensitivity in some dogs, and self/territorial protectiveness.
	9 months	15 years	
	1 year	16 years	
	1.5 years	18 years	
Physical maturity	1.5 years	18 years	Physically looking like adults, but with some youthful tendencies.
	2 years	21 years	
Adult	2 years	21 years	Social maturity The start of having a sensible head on their shoulders. In their prime physically. Developing the doggy wisdom that comes with experience.
	3 years	26 years	
	4 years	31 years	
	5 years	36 years	
	6 years	41 years	
	7 years	46 years	
	9 years	51 years	
Senior	10 years	56 years	Activity levels can drop. Cognitive decline can start to occur. Health problems become more likely. You've shared so much together, you know each other well, these are special years with your companion.
	11 years	61 years	
	12 years	66 years	
	13 years	71 years	
	14 years	76 years	
	15 years	81 years	
	16 years	86 years	
	17 years	91 years	
	18 years	96 years	

CHIHUAHUA, BEAGLE... OR CHEAGLE?

With over 200 dog breeds, and an even larger number of crosses, how do you work out which pup will be right for you?

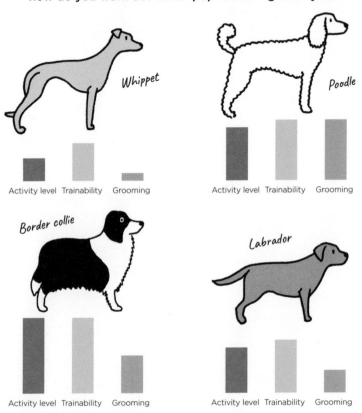

Whippet

Activity level   Trainability   Grooming

Poodle

Activity level   Trainability   Grooming

Border collie

Activity level   Trainability   Grooming

Labrador

Activity level   Trainability   Grooming

HEAD BEFORE HEART

One thing's for sure, it's unlikely you'll be able to resist adopting the first puppy you visit once those adorable eyes meet yours – so do your research before your heart takes over. Ending up with a working Border collie in a tiny flat, or expecting your miniature dachshund to be a marathon training partner, is not what you or your dog would want!

1

Pedigree, crossbreed or mixed-breed?

Do you want pedigree predictability, crossbreed character or mixed-breed magic? An advantage of adopting a pedigree is that you'll have a good idea of their future physical and behavioural attributes. However, crossbreeds (two crossed pedigrees) and mixed-breeds (mixtures of more) often benefit from hybrid vigour – good health and sharp brains! And some crossbreeds have *really* fun names:

Ewokian: Havanese and Pomeranian
Gollie: Golden retriever and collie
Havapoo (yes, really): Havanese and poodle

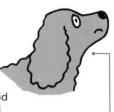

Dogs get up your nose?
If you have allergies, you may want to consider a breed (or crossbreed) that is less allergenic. Poodle, bichon frise and soft-coated wheaten terrier are all good choices.

2

Super-size me

Tiny puppies can grow into huge, powerful adult dogs. Have you got the house and physical strength to manage a mighty giant?

Fur monster
The flowing coat of an Afghan hound may be beautiful, but can you commit to brushing those locks regularly for the next 14 years?

3

Oh behave!

When choosing a breed, behavioural tendencies are more important than looks. Some breeds, such as terriers, have not been bred to follow human directions. Instead, a terrier's job has been to go off independently and kill vermin. If you're after an easily trained, biddable dog, a Jack Russell may not be for you. If you want a dog with character, look no further!

Working for a living
A dog whose ancestors were bred to be workaholics may not cope well with being cooped up inside for much of the day.

THAT DOGGY IN THE WINDOW

Once you've decided on a breed, the next piece of detective work involves where the puppy comes from, which can make a huge difference to their tolerance and sociability in the future.

EARLY EXPERIENCE AND GENETICS

The main things you need to investigate when adopting a puppy are:

- The puppy's early experience.

- The temperaments and health of the puppy's mum and dad.

A puppy that has had a broad range of early experiences will be better set up to cope well with what life may throw at them (see pages 30–31). If you are able to meet both parents – or at least the puppy's mum – and they are relaxed and friendly, this is a good indication the puppy may develop a similar temperament. *If the mum is kept away, walk away!*

1

Chaos is good

The ideal place for a puppy to grow up is at the centre of a busy home. The variety of sights, sounds and social interactions will help your puppy's brain become wired up for tolerance.

Gentling

Picking up puppies daily from a very young age, and handling them carefully, is called gentling. This extra stimulation has been shown to help puppies develop calmer temperaments. It's fantastic if your breeder does this formally, but being handled regularly by a family and visitors will also do the job!

2

Peace can mean problems

Stay clear of adopting puppies from places where they have had a quiet upbringing. Their brains may have been wired to perceive this as normal, and they may struggle with the challenges of the big wide world.

Outbuildings are a red flag

Avoid puppies raised in a farm outbuilding, or in a pedigree show kennel outside. Bear in mind that meeting the puppy inside does not necessarily mean they were raised there, so always check.

3

Medical records

Some pedigree dogs are susceptible to specific health issues. A responsible breeder will do all they can to test for these conditions in their breeding stock. Do your research on the breed, and ask for evidence of relevant genetic tests and veterinary checks on the parents.

Vaccinations and worming

Make sure your puppy has had a health check, first vaccination, and parasite treatment before you take them home.

TO THE RESCUE!

Giving a rescue dog a happy new home, and helping them fulfil their potential, might well be the most rewarding role you can have as a dog guardian.

A CHANCE TO FLOURISH

There are so many unwanted dogs in the world. When you adopt a rescue dog, you are giving them a chance to flourish in a loving home, which is what all dogs want. However, be aware that many dogs are relinquished to shelters because of behavioural issues, or may have had a rough start in life.

This means that some rescue dogs can be more challenging behaviourally than your 'average' dog. Look for rescue centres that have a policy of obtaining and sharing the history of their dogs – they can help you adopt the right dog for your experience and living situation.

1
Time to bloom

After adopting your rescue dog, bear in mind that their immediate behaviour may not represent their long-term behaviour. They may be bringing historical baggage from their previous homes, and the institutionalised experience of rescue kennels. They may also feel a little overwhelmed with the change in scene when moving in with you. Give them time to decompress and you'll see their personality and capability blossom.

The sky's the limit
Just because a dog was abandoned, doesn't mean they have no potential. With your encouragement and patience, it's amazing what new behaviours dogs can learn.

A new beginning
Sometimes it's not possible to find out much about your rescue dog's early life, but knowing you're giving them a new beginning is something special.

2
Retired rescues

If you are after a sedate companion, some lovely older dogs end up being relinquished when their owner passes away. Offering these dogs a quiet retirement home means that you get a close companion while dodging the velociraptor puppy stage.

Call a CAB
If your rescue is showing unwanted behaviour, find a Clinical Animal Behaviourist (CAB) for advice. They have the qualifications and experience to help you.

3
When rescues need rehab

If you begin to experience issues with your rescue dog, it's okay to ask for help. Problems don't mean that you've done anything wrong – each dog comes with its own life story, and you've done a great thing already by bringing them into your family.

FUTURE-PROOF YOUR PUPPY

By getting the early weeks of a puppy's life right, you give them the best chance of a well-adjusted, confident future. If there's one thing a dog wants, it's that!

PUPPY SCHOOL OF LIFE

Puppies emerge into the world with their eyes and ears closed. At this stage life is simple – snuggle for warmth, eat, and let mum lick me to stimulate toileting (and clean it up for me)! After two weeks, a pup's teeth will start to emerge, their eyes and ears will open, and they will begin to stagger about. That's when the learning curve really ramps up – during the next few weeks a puppy may learn more about the world than they will during the rest of their lives. Their brain is soaking in their physical and social environment, and *the more varied their experience is, the more tolerant they will be of new and challenging things as an adult.*

Before your puppy has had its final vaccination at 10–12 weeks, you will need to balance the importance of socialisation with the health risks of encountering disease. Meeting vaccinated dogs in a friend's back garden, carrying your puppy to the shops, and heading out in the car to visit friends with young children are all relatively safe ways to provide your puppy with the experiences they need to grow into a well-adjusted dog.

1

Variety is the spice of life

The period between three and 12 weeks of age is so important for the future confidence of a dog that behaviourists call it the *critical period for socialisation*. Every new person, vaccinated dog, and experience is an investment in your dog's future well-being.

100 Club!
Aim for your puppy to encounter 100 safe places, 100 people and 100 vaccinated dogs by the time they hit 12 weeks of age.

2

How to socialise

You don't need any special techniques to socialise your puppy. It's simple: as long as they don't become overly fearful, all that's required is to give them exposure to different things – new individuals, new places and new experiences.

Puppy parties
Signing up for puppy classes can be a great addition to your puppy's socialisation programme, but to reap the full benefits of broad early experience, ensure you make the effort to socialise your puppy throughout the rest of the week, too!

3

Magic milk and immunity

As with other mammals, the first feed a puppy has from their mum includes colostrum, a super-liquid that helps protect a puppy from disease during their earliest weeks. However, this immunity also interferes with vaccinations, so you can never be sure a puppy is safe until their final vaccination.

Vaccination schedule
With modern vaccines it is possible to finish a puppy's vaccination programme as early as 10 weeks of age. Speak to your vet to see if this is achievable in your area – the sooner your pup is vaccinated, the easier and broader early socialisation can be.

DOGGY DOO-DOOS AND DOGGY DON'TS

One thing that can strain your relationship with your dog is indoor toileting. The good news is that if you get the early weeks right, the jobbie's done.

OUTSIDE IS THE PLACE!

Housetraining your puppy is a combination of teaching them that your home is their den and helping them develop preferences for outdoor toileting surfaces. Get this right and your puppy will forever ask to go outside rather than sneaking behind the couch to do their business.

1

Pee patrol

You need to watch your puppy like a hawk when they're inside, and provide regular trips outside to toilet. Sniffing the ground, circling, whining, and abrupt changes in activity are all signs that it's time to open the door and encourage outdoor business! Every accident indoors is a step in the wrong direction.

It's time to toilet

Puppies toilet at predictable times: after waking, eating, sleeping, playing and excitement. Being aware of these risky moments will help prevent accidents and develop good habits.

Sleep
Toilet
Breakfast
Toilet
Play
Toilet

Pee time, Sweetie!

2

The sacred nest

Most animals have an instinctual dislike of toileting where they rest and eat. Taking advantage of this *nest site inhibition* is the key to housetraining a dog.

Overnight

By having your puppy sleep in a pet crate overnight, and setting an alarm in the middle of the night for you to take them outside, you'll avoid accidents and have a toilet-trained puppy in no time.

3

Puppy pad confusion

'Toileting pads' or newspaper sheets can be an attractive poo or pee place for a puppy who doesn't have an outdoor option, and a tempting solution for an owner to avoid mess on the carpet. But the short-term convenience risks long-term frustration if a dog continues to look for indoor toileting sites once you take the pads away.

Caught with their pants down

If you see your puppy toileting in front of you, interrupt them without frightening them, and quickly take them outside. If you find an existing accident near your puppy, do not tell them off – they won't associate the punishment with the act of toileting indoors so you'll just confuse them and compromise your relationship.

No, no – not on the carpet...

PURPOSEFUL PUPPIES

It's important to have a happily fulfilled puppy – not only is this what your pup wants, it will also minimise headaches for you. Bored pups make their own 'fun', which can actually be frightfully destructive!

THE EVER-FILLING ACTION BATH

Puppies cycle between periods of high-octane lunacy and peaceful, zonked-out sleep. During the action phase it is important to provide appropriate outlets for your pup, so they don't become canine delinquents.

Chewing Granny's reading glasses, digging up your flowers, pulling apart your new rug, none of these is your puppy being 'naughty': your puppy is simply engaging with their world. They might look 'guilty' if we were to tell them off, but this is not guilt: it's actually signalling fear and appeasement to us aggressive humans – which is not the same thing.

Think of your puppy's need for action as a filling bath. If you're not able to drain your pup's 'action-bath', it will overflow into unwanted behaviour.

1

Outlets for your little Chew-barka

Chewing is the number-one puppy desire and you need to fulfil it if you want your home to escape the ravages of *puppydoom*.

Chewie testing

The key to finding the right chew-toy is experimentation. You need to balance durability with destructibility. A rope toy is great for pulling apart; a firmer rubber toy will relieve teething discomfort; a Kong toy delights if you stuff it with frozen goodies – try to provide your puppy with a variety, and go with what they love.

2

Biting and fighting is OK

Puppies *looove* to play-fight and wrestle. By providing appropriate outlets (such as soft rope toys) for this play, you'll prevent your puppy from learning that trouser legs, hands and your mother's cashmere scarf are where the fun's at (see pages 130–31).

Pushing your buttons

Without appropriate outlets for play-fighting, your puppy may not only target undesirable things, but also learn that annoying or even painful biting works to get your attention.

3

Their food is gold

Feeding all of a puppy's daily dry food allowance in a bowl is a wasted opportunity for fun! Weigh out the food, then have the puppy puzzle-solve throughout the day to find it in various ways (see pages 126–7). This gives the puppy important and rewarding work – and helps prevent trouble! For example, scatter a small handful of food across the lawn for a rewarding forage... they'll never know if they've found the last piece!

Puzzle feeders

Look for a rocking puzzle feeder with a weighted bottom and hole near the top that your puppy can knock about to release bits of food (see page 127).

CHAPTER

2

TRAINING
FOR SUCCESS

THE TRUTH ABOUT DOMINANCE

Contrary to popular belief, our dogs are not trying to climb a status ladder towards household domination and 'pack leadership'. Rather, they are more likely to look to us for affection, assistance and fun.

THE DOMINANCE MYTH

Dogs are social creatures like us – they build an understanding of how interactions tend to go within relationships, and then act accordingly. Often a pattern develops between two individual dogs, where one tends to defer to the other when important resources are at stake. If this happens, the dog who normally gets their way is termed 'dominant' within the relationship. But, just because dogs can develop expectations in relationships, it does not mean that they are forever looking for weakness in us, and striving to become the 'Alpha' member of the family. Don't worry, you can sleep peacefully at night in full knowledge that your dog isn't planning a coup d'etat just because you let them sleep on the bed!

1

Wolf studies

The idea dogs are constantly trying to clamber up a hierarchy ladder to become 'pack leader' came from studies in the 1970s where wild wolves, who were unrelated to one another, competed for food in captivity. This high-stress situation didn't represent normal wolf – let alone dog – social behaviour.

A successful meme
Since those unreliable studies in the '70s, the dominance myth has been passed on as received wisdom. For the sake of our dogs, let's work to dispel this meme.

Pack leader? Me?

No need to fight
When people interpret their dog's unwanted behaviour as a 'status' problem, they often try to assert their own 'dominance' through intimidation tactics like rolling the dog over and pinning them down. This can worsen behaviour, confuse or traumatise the dog, and muck up your relationship with them.

2

Dominance blinkers

The dominance myth means we may misinterpret our dog's behaviour as rank-attainment. Aggression? Dominance! Pulling ahead on lead? Dominance! Mouthing the kids? Dominance! This one-size-fits-all assessment can blind us to what is *actually* behind unwanted behaviour. Your dog might be aggressive because they are scared; they might be pulling to get to their friends at the park; and the mouthing of the kids might be just good-natured play.

You're a good boy.

3

Can my dog snooze on the sofa?

Many mini-myths have developed along with the dominance myth. Resting on the sofa, eating before you, or walking out of the door first, say, will not mean your dog starts to think they are 'dominant' and so start to misbehave. These events are a sign of your dog's life preferences unrelated to any concept of social status.

Be a parent not a pack leader
The best way to view your relationship with your dog is as a parent. Sure, boundaries are important, but loving, consistent and fun guidance should be your main focus. Teach your dog how to succeed rather than worrying about being the boss.

LEARN TO EARN

Effective leadership involves teaching your dog that looking to you for direction results in success.

A POWERFUL TECHNIQUE

'Learn to earn' is a lifelong technique where a dog is taught to look to their humans for direction in order to achieve their desires. In practice it means asking a dog to respond to a simple request (such as, sit, down, stay, come) in order to get access to things that they like but that you control. By doing this, you become a guiding facilitator for all the good things in your dog's life, rather than an authoritarian party-pooper!

It's a mindset where a dog thinks 'How can I work with my human to get what I want?', rather than 'What do I have to do to prevent them stopping me doing what I want?', or even worse, 'What action makes them do what I want?'

1

'Learn to earn' in practice

Spot is desperate to get off his lead to play with his doggy friend at the park.

Keep hold of your dog's lead, quietly ask them to 'sit'. Allow your dog to waste their own time if they're not listening, but as soon as your dog does sit, unclip the lead and let them go play.

Pepper wants her ball to be thrown.

Quietly ask for a 'down'. Ignore anything other than a lie-down. Throw the ball as soon as your dog's elbows touch the ground.

Suki wants to rush out of the door for her walk.

Place your hand on the door handle. Ask your dog to 'sit'. Ignore any spinning, standing or barking. Once your dog sits, immediately open the door and allow them to move outside. A more advanced routine would be to ask your dog to stay, and then walk outside before releasing them with an 'OK'.

2

Some things in life should be free

You don't need to be draconian in your use of the 'learn-to-earn' concept – you can give some things in life for free. But, each time you're in a position to withhold something your dog desires, you have an opportunity to teach them that listening pays off!

IS MY NAME 'NO'?

It's human nature to try to deal with misbehaviour when it occurs, but punishment isn't a smart way to train and sours your relationship with your dog.

SET YOUR DOG UP FOR SUCCESS

Dogs want to be taught how to succeed, rather than being scolded constantly. Reduce your need to nag, by setting up your dog's environment to avoid temptation. For example, if your dog loves to 'play tug' with your favourite baggy trousers, put these aside for a few weeks while teaching the dog that sitting in front of you politely often means you will pull out a rope toy – game on!

PUNISHMENT PITFALLS

Reacting to misbehaviour is an amateur way to train because:

> Mum shouts when I bark at the postman. But what else am I meant to do?

This doesn't teach your dog the behaviour you actually *do* want.

> When I want Dad's attention, I bark – he then looks at me and tells me 'no'. Any attention is good attention!

Your reaction may unintentionally reward the unwanted behaviour.

> Mum and Dad say 'no' so often it just fades into the background.

Your dog may desensitise to your nagging and learn to ignore you.

> I get nervous spending time with Grandma because she's scary.

If your dog gets stressed when told off, you might damage your relationship with them, especially if they don't understand why they are being told off.

THE MAGIC OF PLAY

Play is an important social glue that cements a close relationship with your dog. If there's one thing most dogs want, it's more play!

PLAY HAS A PURPOSE

We all love a fun game with our dogs, but did you know play has many benefits?

- Play cements humans as key social partners.

- Play helps a puppy's brain develop so that they can deal with frustration better as they mature, and therefore have better impulse control.

- Play develops physical coordination.

- Play builds and maintains your relationship with your dog. Families who play together thrive together!

- Play releases feel-good endorphins. Just what your dog wants – a healthy buzz! This can provide an emotional buffer to life's stresses.

- Play provides appropriate outlets for your dog – keeping them out of trouble!

1

Breeds and play preferences

We each have our favourite sports, and it's the same with our dogs. Terriers often love nothing better than a vigorous game of tug, sighthounds relish a game of chase-and-be-chased, and collies delight in 'herding' and ball retrieval.

Reluctant retrievers
Many dogs love the thrill of chasing a ball, but once they have their 'prey', they are reluctant to turn it over to us. So frustrating! A good way to reform a reluctant retriever is to use two balls of the same type. Once the first is thrown, load up with the second, wait for your dog to return, and as soon as they drop the first ball throw the second – *you must give to receive!*

2

Catch me if you can!

An all-time play favourite with many dogs involves chasing and being chased. Try this: freeze and give your dog a crazy look, race away from them at top speed before stopping suddenly and planting your hands on the ground. Pause for a second before racing away again, turn and start to chase them as if you're playing tag. Collapse exhausted!

3

Keep calm and carry on

Some dogs can become so keyed up when playing that they go overboard. Whatever the game, it can be useful to stop, request a sit, then continue only once your dog sits and settles.

Watch the experts
Channel your inner David Attenborough and study how dogs at your local park play with each other. Let go of your inhibitions and play like a canine with your dog at home – they'll love you for it!

Pause to play
Periodic 'pause to play' is a great way to teach your dog that calming on cue almost always guarantees that the fun will continue, and is a useful routine to turn down the heat of play if needed.

LEARNING ABOUT LEADS

Leads provide a golden thread between you and your dog,
and they offer many benefits.

WHY USE A LEAD?

- Leads keep your dog safe.

- Being on-lead is a legal requirement in some areas.

- A lead allows you to manage your dog without constantly giving them verbal cues (which can desensitise a dog to your requests).

- Leads allow you to prevent or interrupt unwanted behaviour easily (like eating dead birds, jumping on strangers, or running off to chase animals).

- A lead enables you to teach your dog that desirable behaviour pays off.

A LEAD FOR EVERY OCCASION

Umbilical – a 2m-long lead that clips around your waist. Great for hands-free training; for example, for toilet training a puppy or when you're going for a run.

House-line – around 2.5m long, this is a lightweight line with no loop at the end, left to drag about behind your dog while under supervision. You can pick it up when you need to control your dog – an excellent no-nonsense and non-confrontational way to interrupt unwanted behaviour and prompt desirable behaviour.

Long-line – at 10m long, this is freedom with control but requires a little practice to master. It's great for when you want to retain control of your dog but give them a chance to engage in doggy pursuits in larger outdoor areas. You can drop it and let your dog drag it in some situations. Attach it to a harness rather than a collar.

Conventional – at 2m long with a loop handle and a clip to attach to a collar or harness, this lead is good for tight spaces, and is convenient and not too bulky. It's long enough for your dog to sniff things on the footpath without wandering on to the road or tripping passers-by.

Retractable lead – a 5–8m-long lead with the main benefit that the long line feeds in and out automatically from the plastic handle. This can cause problems, however, as controlling your dog this way is less intuitive than with a standard long-line, and the handle can sometimes pop out of your hand and 'chase' your dog – very stressful!

COLLARS, HARNESSES AND HEADCOLLARS

Dogs don't come with a built-in attachment point for a lead – so what are the options?

> I do like to accessorise.

KEEP IT KIND

In days gone by, noose-type devices were the collars of choice for many dog owners. But they acted by tightening around a dog's neck causing discomfort and injury – particularly with the 'checks' or yanks advocated by old-fashioned trainers. Fortunately, there are more enlightened options now – more along the lines of what your dog might want if they were able to choose.

1
Flat collar

Pros: Convenient. A flat collar can stay on a dog ready for you to clip on a lead at any time, and it will hold your dog's ID tag 24/7.

Con: Can put pressure on delicate parts of the throat and neck, risking injury if a dog pulls hard against it.

Houdini dogs...
Some dogs with muscular necks or pin-heads can slip out of their collar at moments of high excitement! By using a martingale collar, which tightens slightly but not enough to choke, you have a collar that can stay loose on a dog's neck, but safely tighten up to prevent a slippery wriggle for freedom.

2
Harness

Pros: Lowest risk of causing injury to your dog if well fitted. Useful if you want your dog to pull you (such as for Canicross or sledding) – just attach your lead to the back of the harness and fly!

Cons: Not suitable to leave on all the time, so you need to take a harness on and off as required. Can cause chafing if poorly fitted or left on too long. More comfortable than a flat collar for your dog to pull into because the attachment point is usually on their back... so if you DON'T want them to pull (and very likely you don't), you need to make sure your training is on-point, or use a harness with a front attachment.

Harnesses for dogs who pull
Choose a harness with a D-ring at the chest rather than on the back – this can give you more control as it will help you turn their body when required.

3
Headcollar

Pros: Excellent control – where the head goes the body follows! No direct pressure on the neck.

Cons: Dogs, like most animals, can take time to get used to having something on their face, so you may need to commit to some adjustment training.

Headcollar hints...
Try the Halti, Gentle Leader or Dogmatic brands with the lead attachment point under the chin. It's important to select the right size, adjust it correctly, and make sure your dog receives lots of small super-treats initially when not pawing at it. If your dog is rubbing or pawing at the head-collar, have a little tension on the lead so they can't slip it off, but be ready to immediately give slack when they leave it alone. Slack = success!

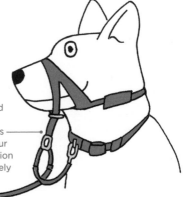

THE MUZZLE PUZZLE

Muzzles can look intimidating, and we humans can be judgemental about dogs wearing them, but wearing a muzzle can actually lead to a happier dog.

> Finally! Some personal space!

MUZZLE BENEFITS

Granted, muzzles aren't the cutest bits of doggy equipment, and many people are very reluctant to use them, but a muzzle can really benefit a reactive dog. Many dogs bite when they get stressed, and while you might understand your dog's needs and act appropriately, you can't always control the environment around you. Importantly, muzzles help keep everyone safe, which also means you and your dog are less likely to get in trouble with the law. A muzzle is a very clear sign to people that your dog needs space – for socially sensitive dogs this can be a huge relief, and walks in public often become far less stressful. Wearing a muzzle can also mean you can give your reactive dog a little more freedom than you might otherwise.

1

Basket vs fabric muzzles

Basket muzzles might look unappealing, but they can offer important benefits compared to slip-on fabric tube muzzles. Significantly, they allow your dog to pant, which is critical for keeping cool and getting plenty of oxygen. In contrast, many fabric muzzles keep a dog's mouth nearly closed, which is not what your dog wants when they are hot or exercising.

Look for:
- Design and size to ensure the muzzle can't slip off.
- Comfort in the fit – no pressure points.
- A broad and/or soft area to rest on the nose.
- Is your dog able to pant and drink?
- A hole in the front big enough to post treats through.

Treat time! Yippee!

Will my dog think they're being punished?
If you only ever put a muzzle on your dog during stressful situations, eventually they'll run a mile whenever they see one. On the other hand, if they know it signifies treats and a walk, they'll be running towards the muzzle like a heat-seeking missile!

2

My party hat

You can help your dog learn to love their muzzle by making sure that each time the muzzle goes on, their favourite food titbits come out. If wearing a muzzle predicts good times, it becomes a party hat rather than a dunce cap.

3

What will people think?

People who understand dogs will think you're great because you're keeping things safe, and looking after your dog. Good on you, a muzzle is a sign of a responsible dog guardian.

Thanks for the opportunity
If your fearful dog is wearing a muzzle, you can very carefully introduce them to new people and dogs to build their social skills and tolerance in a safe and responsible way. (See also pages 152-3.)

HOW DOGS LEARN

All animals learn in fundamentally the same way – by linking actions to outcomes. Dogs are no exception.

OUTCOMES CHANGE BEHAVIOUR

Dogs learn 'by association' – their behaviour changes as a result of outcomes.

It's simple: if they link a certain behaviour with feeling good (or feeling relieved), they will do it more often. On the other hand, if they associate that behaviour with bad things happening (or the end of good times), they are less likely to repeat it.

Understanding this will help you teach your dog to be a model canine citizen – in a form they would choose themselves if they could.

THE LEARNING QUADRANTS

The 'learning quadrants' below summarise how dogs learn. Avoid old-fashioned training techniques that use discomfort or intimidation to compel behaviour: these can scare, confuse and stress your dog, and risk damaging your relationship with them. As an enlightened trainer, you'll be helping your dog learn via 'positive reinforcement' (the top-left quadrant) – teaching them to repeat behaviour that results in wonderful outcomes! (The bottom-right quadrant can be useful at specific times, too – see page 139.)

BEHAVIOUR INCREASES

Good stuff happens	Bad stuff stops

 YAY!

 PHEW! He's stopped pinching my toes!

Learning to keep feet on the floor because it brings good stuff.

Learning to keep feet on the floor to avoid bad stuff.

Bad stuff happens	Good stuff stops

 OUCH!

DAMN! Pats stopped.

Learning not to jump up as it brings bad stuff.

Learning not to jump up as it causes the good stuff to stop.

BEHAVIOUR DECREASES

BE PROACTIVE NOT REACTIVE

If there's one secret to training a well-behaved dog, it's to *proactively* teach them that good behaviour pays off, rather than *reactively* jumping on them for unwanted behaviour. Use brain not brawn!

TAKE THE INITIATIVE

Modern dog training is all about *motivation* not intimidation. By making a little effort each day to think about the types of behaviour you want, and taking the initiative to ensure this behaviour pays off for your dog regularly, you'll be ahead of 90% of dog owners. Rather than thinking 'How do I stop my dog doing this or that', think 'What is it that I want my dog *to do*?', and then look for opportunities to reward for this behaviour.

1

Invest in the basics

In our busy lives we can end up trying to train our dogs on the fly, amid the chaos and while they are distracted. This sets you and your dog up to fail. Set aside five minutes a day exclusively to teach and practise basic cues, and you'll soon see amazing results.

Don't overcook it
Keep your 5-minute training sessions focused, fun and to the point. Don't be tempted to push on through if your dog starts losing interest!

2

The treat allowance

A good way to remind yourself to reward your dog for their good behaviour is to have a daily allowance of ten small food treats that you need to 'spend' randomly through the day by asking your dog to do things you've covered in training. If you get to the end of the day and you've still got treats left, you'll need to do better tomorrow!

Spread the love
Give everyone a daily allowance of treats to reward your dog with – that means each household member becomes a dog trainer! The kids can have five when they get back from school; maybe Grandad has come for a visit and he wants a go, too...

3

They can't be bad if they're good

Rather than focusing on punishing an unwanted behaviour, take the initiative to train a desirable behaviour that makes the unwanted one impossible. For example, a dog can't jump if they're sitting down!

Leaping lizards – it's a visitor!
If your dog jumps up at visitors, keep a box of treats by the front door, and explain to guests that they can give a reward or two if Fido is sitting patiently to greet them.

THE ABC OF TRAINING

Knowing your training ABC will help you train like a pro.

ASK > BEHAVIOUR > CONSEQUENCE!

Successful training begins with A,B,C...

First, you'll *ask*...

Next, your dog completes the *behaviour*...

Then, there's a *consequence*.

Whatever you do, don't forget to make it to C – it's the consequence that will change or maintain your dog's behaviour in the future. If you only ask, and never provide a meaningful outcome, the behaviour will fall apart! Who can be bothered if there's no real benefit to listening?

1

Reward frequency

When your dog is learning something new, it helps to keep their confidence up by rewarding every success – dogs want to know they're on the right track. However, once they understand what you're after, it's better *not* to reward every time. Intermittent rewards help to improve the *consistency* of a dog's response.

Nice rollover!

Perfection pays off
Not only do intermittent rewards keep your dog sharp, but it also means you can selectively reward your dog for their most polished performances, which encourages long-term poochy perfection.

2

The missing link

Do you find your dog sometimes runs through a loop of tricks instead of just responding to your cue? 'Behaviour flurries' happen when the link between A and C is unclear. Your dog thinks that if they run through everything, they'll eventually hit on the right response. It's the canine equivalent of mashing all the buttons on a computer game!

Sit! Bark! Paw! I'm so confused!

Ace it to earn it
To avoid the issue of behaviour flurries, reward your dog only when they immediately do the exact behaviour you asked for, rather than if they perform it somewhere within a sequence of tricks.

3

Achievable training

Start off easy when you're teaching your dog a new behaviour. If you intend to set a university-level challenge, make sure they've got their head around the earlier school grades first so they don't get disheartened. By building on success, you can gradually increase the challenge.

Distraction proofing
Once your dog knows a behaviour, you'll need to practise it in various different situations to 'proof' them against distractions such as other dogs and people and other things *liiike... SQUIRREL!*

THE INS AND OUTS OF FOOD REWARDS

There are many prizes you can use to congratulate your dog, but you're missing a trick (and so might your dog!) if you seldom surprise them with a food reward.

REWARDING WITH FOOD

Dogs repeat behaviour that has paid off for them in the past. One currency we can use to 'pay' most dogs is food – it's a powerful and practical unit of reward.

Treats are very useful when you're teaching your dog new behaviour, and can also motivate them to do good stuff that they already know.

While some dogs do love other prizes more than food (chasing a ball or playing tug games), food rewards are an essential part of your training toolbox!

1

Don't get stuck in a food rut

When you're teaching your dog something new, it's okay to have the food right there: you might be using a 'luring technique' to help them learn (see pages 66–7), and also it means you can reward quickly to help them understand when they've succeeded. But after that, you want to surprise them with food rather than bribing.

Great work, Daisy! What do I have here?

Surprise don't bribe
Reach for the food reward *after* your dog responds, rather than *before*.

No treats – ignore!

The human test
Can your friends or family tell if you are going to reward your dog – maybe you are holding a piece of food in your hand, or rustling the packet in your pocket. If your family can tell, so can your dog!

2

'My dog listens only if I offer a treat'

Good news! This is a common, solvable training issue. Start making it a mystery whether or not you'll reward your dog with a treat. Before long, they'll realise it's always worth listening to your cues – even when there's no sign of a snack.

3

A safe bet

Rewarding should be like playing a slot machine – your dog will never know when a pay-off will occur, but they'll always respond to you in the hope that it will!

Jackpot!
Your dog will be extra-keen if you occasionally provide an amazing jackpot surprise – like a cat-food sachet, or some meaty leftovers.

Yes! It's the big one!

WHY FOOD REWARDS WORK

Let's address a few age-old concerns that often hold people back from using food rewards. That way, we can make sure there are no bits of fluff in our otherwise perfect training toolbox.

WILL MY DOG STILL RESPECT ME?

There used to be a theory that dogs should respect our 'commands' without needing food to encourage them. This came from the old-fashioned idea that dogs are best trained through intimidation, rather than motivation. It's not true! If listening to you means the choicest parts of your dog's daily food rations are up for grabs, your dog will respect you all the more.

1

'My dog isn't food motivated'

All dogs are motivated by food to some degree – otherwise they wouldn't have survived this long! If your dog has a take-it-or-leave-it attitude to food, there are things you can do change the 'Meh' to 'Yeah!'

Not all food rewards are created equal

Your dog may turn their nose up at a dry biscuit but do back-flips for liver-cake. Making an effort to use scrumptious food rewards, such as cheese, sausage and chicken, can make all the difference. Prepare a big pile of these super-rewards, cut into tiny pieces. You can freeze handfuls in individual bags ready for action!

Stop jazzing up dinner

If your dog is a little fussy, resist the temptation to jazz up their main meal with special titbits – save these as food rewards.

Lean means keen

Check your dog is at their ideal weight (see page 97). If they are overweight, gradually reduce their daily food until they're a healthy weight – this will help turn their stomach on to food, and benefit their health in the long run, too.

End free-feeding

If your dog has access to a bowl of food throughout the day, foodie rewards may not motivate them. It's all about supply and demand – lift that food bowl once they walk away from it and the treats will be *deeeelicious*!

2

A weighty issue

Many people are concerned that using food treats will super-size their dog. You can easily avoid this by cutting up rewards into tiny pieces, and reducing their daily food allowance a little so that their food treats + daily food ration = daily calorific requirements.

Gently does it...

If your dog snatches at food in your hand, teach them to take it more gently. Hold the reward in your fist, and open your hand only once they're gentle. Snatchy = fail; gentle = success. Giving the food from the palm of your hand can be easier on the fingers with some sharky types.

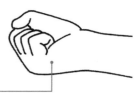

CLICKER CLARITY

The humble-looking clicker is actually an extremely useful training tool. It helps your dog figure out which behaviours pay off. Training clarity is what a dog wants!

SO, WHAT'S A CLICKER?

A clicker is just a small plastic box with a metal flap that makes a clear 'click' sound when you press it. Initially the sound is meaningless to a dog. But if you follow every click with a small super-treat, it soon becomes meaningful: a click predicts a food reward!

Once your dog has learned that a 'click' has meaning, you can use it to show them exactly which behaviours earn them a reward. *This is a clicker's real power – it helps your dog make a link between the desired behaviour and the wonderful pay-off of food.*

1

A bridge to success

Think of the clicker as a promise to your dog – a click means 'That's it! A treat is coming!' It's a bridge between the desired behaviour and the reward, a marker of success.

Timing is everything
It's the timing of the click that is important, rather than how quickly you get the food reward to your dog afterwards. Once your dog understands that a click means a reward, you can take a couple of seconds to produce the prize.

2

2

Training humans too!

A clicker is brilliant for you as a trainer. It encourages you to think more clearly about the precise behaviour you're asking of your dog, because you're focused on clicking at the exact moment they succeed.

Shaping behaviour
Once you've got the basics down, you can use a clicker for more complex behaviours – like teaching your dog to put all their toys away in the basket. To do this, you'll need to break the behaviour into small, trainable steps. Use the clicker to precisely mark each small step and build towards the final behaviour. This training process is called 'shaping'.

Step 1: holding toy

Step 2: dropping toy

Step 3: holding and...

...dropping toy

Step 4: taking one by one...

...and dropping one by one

3

A click is not for ever

As soon as your dog knows the behaviour you're looking for, and is responding reliably on cue, you can stop using the clicker for this behaviour.

Don't forget to pay
Once you teach your dog a behaviour, you won't need the precision of a clicker any more, although you will still need to motivate them with surprise rewards.

I don't think I need this any more.

SIT

So simple, so effective... let's train a sit!

A PAUSE BUTTON FOR YOUR DOG

A consistent 'sit' is a really valuable behaviour to establish with your dog. It's your dog's pause button.

A sit allows you to ask that your dog park themselves for a bit, so that you can sort out the situation. It might keep them safe while waiting at a busy road, or help prevent an over-enthusiastic bum-wag from knocking over your niece, or make clipping a lead to their collar less like catching a fly with chopsticks.

1

Training a sit

While your dog is standing, hold a tasty piece of food in front of their nose, and then slowly lift it up and slightly backwards towards their ears. Your dog's nose will follow the food up and their bum should ease down to the floor taking them into the sit position. Give them the food as soon as their rear end touches the ground.

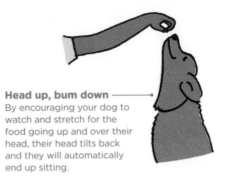

Head up, bum down
By encouraging your dog to watch and stretch for the food going up and over their head, their head tilts back and they will automatically end up sitting.

2

Jumping Jacks

If your dog jumps for the food, quickly move the treat out of reach and try again. Your dog will soon learn that jumping up is a waste of time and energy, whereas a sit pays off!

Keep it positive
There's no need to say 'uh-uh' or 'no' if your dog doesn't succeed during the head-up-bum-down phase. You want them to be relaxed rather than worried about getting it wrong. During the learning phase, help your dog to feel at ease to try out different behaviours, so they will keep trying until they hit on the behaviour you want.

Mark with a 'yes'
Whenever you want to reward desirable behaviour, say 'Yes!' before you reach for a reward. This will become a valuable signal to your dog that they are doing what you want (you could also use a clicker; see pages 62–3).

3

Minimise the cue

Once your dog will consistently sit when your hand is moved over their head, simplify the gesture: increase the height of your hand above your dog's head, and reward them after they sit. Soon you'll be able to simply bring a closed hand to your chest, and your dog will understand this as 'sit'. At this point you can also introduce 'sit' as a verbal cue.

LIE DOWN

A trained lie-down is another very useful 'pause' button for your dog, but it can be tricky to establish at first. Here's a technique that works with 99% of dogs.

DOGGY YOGA

Begin training the lie-down with your dog sitting on a smooth surface. Hold some enticing squidgy food between your fingers, with only a little bit of the food showing.

Slowly lower your hand down towards the floor, allowing your dog to nibble at the food. You want to encourage them to stretch downwards into a slightly unnatural position – an awkwardness that they will relieve when they relax into the lie-down.

As they nibble away, gradually squish a little more food through your fingers to help motive them to engage in this doggy yoga rather than giving up. When your dog brings their paws forwards and both elbows touch the ground – BINGO! Congratulate them with a 'Yes!' and allow them to take the remaining food.

1
Avoiding a stand-off

If your dog starts to stand up instead of lying down, quickly pull the food away, ask them to sit, and start again. In the early stages, some dogs need a gentle hand on their rear end as a hint to keep their bum on the ground while you lower the treat, but avoid this if you can.

The Goldilocks Zone
The position of your hand is critical. If your hand is too close to your dog, they'll want to stand (or maybe they won't need to stretch enough to complete the lie-down), but if it's too far away they'll simply give up trying or be more inclined to stand. Your hand position needs to be *juuuust* right as you lower it to the floor.

2

2
The next stage

Once your dog is lying down nine times out of ten, move on to the next stage: use the same gesture, but with your hand closed to hide the food. As soon as their elbows touch the ground, say 'Yes!' and open your hand.

Clear signals
It's easier for your dog to understand if you use consistent verbal and visual 'cues' for the behaviours you train. At stage 2 you can calmly start to say the word 'down' as a verbal cue for your dog to enter the lie-down.

3
Training complete

The final stage is to gesture with an empty hand. As soon as your dog's elbows touch the ground, say 'Yes!' then drop a treat on to the previously empty hand and allow your victorious dog to take it. They'll realise that even if they can't see a treat, there might still be a pay-off when they respond to your 'down' cue.

Still struggling?
If you are having trouble with getting a lie-down, try the 'all-or-nothing' technique. Simply wait for moments through the day when your dog lies down near you, before saying 'Yes!' and reaching for a treat. You can then start to develop a link between your 'down' cue and a lie-down!

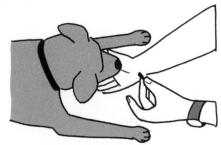

RECALL

Coming back when called is what trainers refer to as 'recall'. This important behaviour is easy to train – but harder to maintain!

TRAINING THE RECALL

When you begin training recall, start off in an environment with no distractions.

Stash a small super-treat between the thumb and palm of your hand. Tap your thighs with your hands and call out a crisp, fun-sounding 'Come!' while taking a few steps backwards. As your dog approaches you, turn your hand to reveal the food and give it to them along with lots of excited praise, and a congratulatory chest and shoulder rub. Trot backwards again and repeat. Once your dog has the hang of this, wait until they are slightly distracted before calling and – with success – rewarding again. That's the recall taught, but it's only the start of a lifetime of recall maintenance!

1

Competing with distractions

The attractions of the big wide world can really interfere with a dog's recall. You need to teach your dog that coming back is the bee's knees, rather than a drag.

Come!

Boost the benefit, cut the cost
Think about maxing out the pay-off to your dog for coming back (such as super-treats or play), while reducing the cost to them (that their fun stops).

Good boy, find it!

Scatter and seek
A 'find it' foraging game is a great way to make delicious recall rewards even more exciting.

2

Max-out the motivation

Sometimes your dog will be interested in tempting distractions that are tough to compete with. For this reason, it's important to use top-tier food rewards with the recall. Ditch boring biscuits, and surprise your dog with good stuff like frankfurter, cheese, chicken or liver-cake. With some dogs a surprise ball-throw or game of tug will super-charge their motivation.

3

Using a whistle

A whistle is a fantastic cue for the recall. It's clear and consistent and carries over a distance. You don't need a special dog whistle – just make sure you can replace whichever you choose with one that sounds the same, if need be!

A reminder for us
Using a whistle is helpful for you as a trainer because you know in your mind that it has a very specific purpose and you're less likely to overuse it. (You don't want your dog to start treating 'Come!' as meaningless white noise because you've shouted it one too many times without meaning it!)

REBUILD YOUR RECALL

If your dog has an inconsistent recall, sometimes it's because they think there might be a 'cost' to coming back.

ARE YOU HAVING RECALL ISSUES?

Does your dog become 'deaf' when called? This is a really common problem! When your dog's having fun off-lead and you call them, their mind doesn't consider what's right or wrong – just 'What works out best for me?' If they ignore you, their fun continues; but if they come back, they're 'punished' because they lose access to their fun. (And if you manage to catch them or trick them, they'll learn from your wily ways and try to outwit you next time.) The good news is you can get your recall back on the right track with a few top tips.

1

Feeling positive

Coming back to you should be a rewarding detour for your dog, not a dead-end. Make sure that you pay them for it and, if you can, let them go back to what they were doing so they don't think recall means the fun has to end. Show them you're not just a spoilsport!

Good girl, you can go back and play again now.

Let the fun continue

Every time you have to call your dog away from something they aren't allowed to go back to (such as snuffling around that other family's delicious picnic), aim to make up for it with at least five return-to-fun recalls.

2

Consider a long-line

Often it's all or nothing with recall training – your dog's either on-lead and tightly controlled, or off-lead and free as a bird to ignore you. If you use a long-line (see page 47), you'll be able to retain control of Mr Ropey Recall, but give him the freedom to be able to run about. This will help you practise the recall in a natural but controlled way.

Let the line do the work

Use the long-line (without saying anything) to guide your dog away from undesirable activities. Save the recall as much as possible for when coming back will be a positive outcome for your dog. That way, recall signals good times, rather than boring 'Stop your fun!'

Disappearing act

If your dog ignores your recall and you're in a safe area, quickly move away and hide. Most dogs will become concerned at your disappearance and actively begin a search-and-rescue operation! Now your dog's learning that it's on them to maintain contact with you – rather than the other way around.

3

White noise

Don't repeat 'Come!' over and over if your dog is distracted and appears to be ignoring you. Doing so will just turn your voice into meaningless white noise! Instead, the best thing is to take hold of your dog and clip them back on their lead. Save recall practice for later, when there are fewer distractions and you're both feeling more relaxed and attentive.

STAY

Training your dog to stay put is one of the most useful things you can teach them to do, but it does take practice.

THE FOUNDATIONS OF A ROCK-SOLID STAY

The key to training a 'stay' is to start off easily, with no distractions. Ask your dog to 'sit', then extend your palm to them and calmly say 'stay' – *the stay has now started* and your dog should not get up until you release them with 'OK'. Slowly take half a step backwards, and before your dog is tempted to move, return and reward them with a small treat. Repeat.

Once your dog has the hang of this, increase the distance you retreat to a full step, then a full step with a one-second pause. If your dog starts to stand, say 'ah' quietly *as soon as they start to stand*, and ask them to sit-stay again. Slowly progress to greater distances and longer pauses; increase distractions, walk around them, and try moving to another room, then watch them through a crack in the door. Whatever stage you are at, the same rules apply: between the 'stay' and the 'OK', your dog must not stand!

1

Successful steps

If your dog will stay put at a certain level for five out of five goes, you're both ready to increase the challenge: try a longer distance, bigger pause, more distractions. If they're staying 4/5 times, carry on at the current level. If they're succeeding 3/5 times or fewer, decrease the challenge until they've really nailed the basics.

'Freeze'
Consider using an unusual word such as 'freeze' instead of 'stay'. This reminds you to focus on the task!

Supervision is key
Use 'stay' only if you have the time to monitor your dog.

2

Practice makes perfect

Before using the stay in tricky situations (and suffering that embarrassing moment when your dog runs gleefully past you anyway), practise like a pro! For example, train your dog to stay in the car as you open the door while it's parked in your driveway, before expecting a stay when you arrive at a busy car park at the start of a favourite walk.

Clap for clarity
To make sure the moment of release is clear for your dog (and you). Clap your hands twice as you release them with 'OK'.

3

Release the hounds

If you ask your dog to stay, remember to always release them with 'OK'. (Each time your dog breaks the stay themselves, they are learning that your 'stay' doesn't really mean stay – it means 'I might let you get up if you give it a go.')

KEEP MOTIVATED

Teaching your dog the core four cues of sit, down, come and stay is important – but they are only the start. If you live with a dog, every day is a training day!

FINDING THEIR PASSION

Training doesn't stop just because your dog recognises a cue such as 'sit'. You need them to be motivated to actually *do* what you ask whenever you ask it. Here's a tip: use their passion to pay them! Make an effort to surprise your dog with rewards that are really meaningful for them.

1 'He knows what to do, he's just not doing it!'

Your dog will learn to sit quickly. But they're going to become reluctant sitters if there's never much of a pay-off after the learning phase. You can easily turn up your dog's enthusiasm by becoming a generous tipper!

All I ever get is a pat? Meh!

'But I praise my dog!'
You can't blame your dog for dragging their paws if their only motivation is a measly pat on the head. Would you do your job for praise only?

Endless possibilities
Sometimes you won't reward your dog for their responsiveness at all; at other times you might surprise them with their very, very, *very* favourite thing.

2 Mystery is motivating

You don't need to reward your dog every time they respond to a cue. In fact it's the mystery of the good things that *might* happen that really keeps a dog's responses sharp.

Proper praise
Patting your dog on their head with a donk-donk-donk-type pat is not much of a reward. In fact, most dogs don't like it at all. Proper praise involves excited, high-pitched verbal praise, and a lovely big rub on their chest and shoulders or a satisfying scratch around their ears and cheeks, or at the base of their tail.

3 Fun times

The best rewards aren't always edible! Often it's about surprising dogs with the chance to do something they love. That might be a toy to shake if your dog is a terrier, a 'find-it' game for your Australian shepherd, or a chase game for your collie. Turn the page for some more ideas...

PAY WITH FUN!

Rewards aren't just for special occasions – and there's more to them than just food treats...

Good boy! Walkies!

LEVERAGE LIFE'S PLEASURES

As part of your life with your dog, you'll do lots of lovely things for them. Make the most of these interactions for training purposes! For example, instead of giving away that it's walk-time by putting on your coat and grabbing the lead, you can use the upcoming walk as a reward for listening to you.

Before you give any hint you're taking your dog to their favourite park, ask them for a behaviour they know (such as 'bed'). When they do as you ask (in this case, go to their bed), surprise them with an excited 'Yes! WALKIES!' Then, head straight for the door, picking up the lead on the way.

1

Chews wisely

If you're going to give your dog a dental chew each day, don't just give it at the same time – what a wasted opportunity! Instead *surprise* them with it after they respond to one of your regular requests.

Chase up good behaviour

If your dog loves the chase-and-be-chased game (see page 45), you might ask them to sit, then surprise them with a thrilling bout of chase when they do it!

Absence makes the heart grow fonder

Toy rotation maximises your dog's interest in that day's toys, as they won't have seen them for a while!

Oh, wow! I've missed you Mr Piggy!

2

Mixing it up

Rather than leaving out all your dog's toys, keep out only two or three at a time, rotating them with a different selection every few days. Bringing out a toy from storage can be a surprise reward for good behaviour.

Tug surprise

Some dogs just live for their next tug session. When your dog does a beautiful 'down' for you, try rewarding that tenacious tugger with a rope-toy from your pocket.

3

No such thing as a free lunch

Every mealtime is actually a bonus training opportunity. Before you prepare your dog's food, ask them to do something for you. For example, call them to a random room in the house and ask them to sit. When they do, say 'Dinnertime!' and head off together to fix up that food.

Good boy!

CHAPTER

3

INSIDE A DOG'S MIND

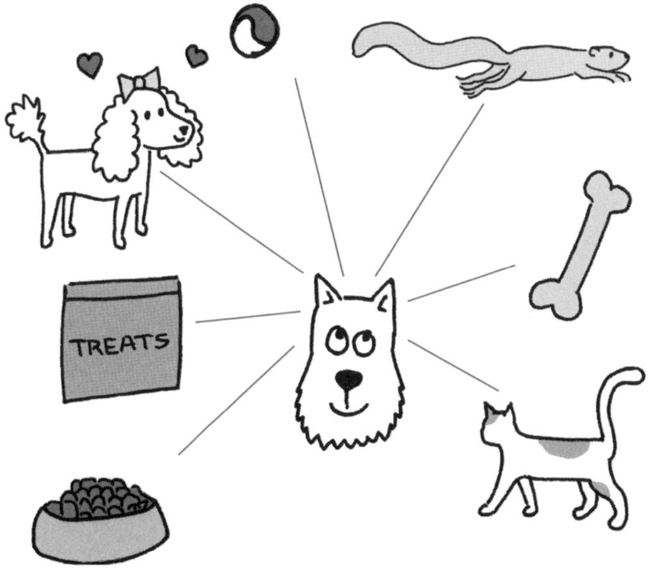
TREATS

THE TAIL TELLS A TALE

A dog's tail reveals so much about their emotional state and intentions. Here's the low-down on what your dog's tail is telling you.

THE SURPRISING TRUTH

A waggy tail means a happy dog, right? Nope, not necessarily. It just means the dog is aroused – and arousal can be driven by different emotions. You need to take account of what the rest of your dog's body is doing in order to read the meaning in the wag. Yes, your dog might be totally brimming with happy excitement, but the wag *could* *instead* indicate anything from annoyed frustration to adrenaline-fuelled worry – or any combo of these emotions! *The quicker a dog wags its tail, the more intense their feelings.*

The exception is the 'helicopter tail' or 'propeller wag' – an enthusiastic rotating tail and bum waggle – which normally means a happy dog!

Above or below the line?

Another key indicator of how your dog is feeling is where they are holding their tail. A tail that points just downwards compared to the line of the spine tends to mean a relaxed dog. The higher your dog raises their tail above this point, the higher their arousal or confidence. The lower the tail, the more worried or unconfident they are.

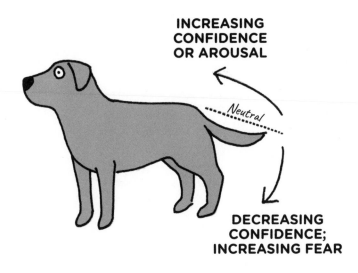

INCREASING CONFIDENCE OR AROUSAL

Neutral

DECREASING CONFIDENCE; INCREASING FEAR

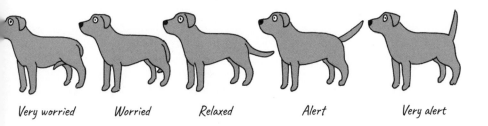

Very worried   *Worried*   *Relaxed*   *Alert*   *Very alert*

Tail accents

Each dog has their own tail 'accent', with some dogs tending to hold their tail higher, some lower. This might be their personality shining through, but can also be down to their breed. For example, spitz breeds (like Alaskan malamutes) tend to hold their tails very high, while sighthounds (like whippets) are often low-riders!

READ MY FACE

Dogs have such expressive faces. Here are some tips to help you understand how your dog might be feeling – from the positive, through the negative, to the 'Achoo!'

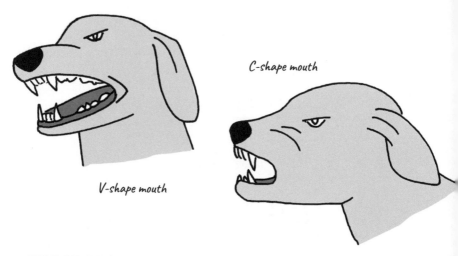

C-shape mouth

V-shape mouth

THOSE PEARLY WHITES

Some mouth positions take a trained eye to interpret – and for a spot-on translation it's important to read the rest of a dog's body language, too.

One signal that tends to be pretty cut and dried is when a dog draws their lips up to show their teeth. This is a clear warning that they are not comfortable with a situation – if push came to shove, they could bite. Did you know that when a dog bares their teeth, the corners of their mouth say a lot about their confidence? If your dog draws the corners forward to make a 'C' shape, you are witnessing an aggressive pucker that represents a confident threat or warning. If the dog draws the corners back into a 'V' shape (so the lips are tight), the dog is less confident (the teeth-baring is probably driven primarily by fear). Either dog could bite, but a dog with the C might be more self-assured and proactive about it, while a dog with the V might bite only as a last resort.

1

Eyes – hard or soft?

A dog's eyes can be a window to their soul. A hard, fixed stare can indicate building tension and stress: give them space, especially if they freeze, growl or lift a lip!

2

Neutral ears

Dog ears come in all shapes and sizes, from small and pricked, to long and dangly. If you know where your dog's ears tend to sit when they're relaxed, you'll be in a good position to figure out what the angle of the dangle means.

Happy face
A dog with soft eyes and slightly droopy lids, and a relaxed mouth, is most likely calm and happy.

3

Alert

Neutral

Worried or less confident

Scared or appeasing

Forward or flat?
If your dog's ears are rotated forward and held high on their head, the dog is likely to be alert or feeling confident. If the ears are rotated back, your dog may be worried, lacking confidence or trying to indicate they mean no harm. The further back a dog's ears are rotated, the more worried they are likely to be.

3

'Damn-it' sneeze

Ever wonder why your dog sneezes when excited? This is a 'damn-it' sneeze, brought about by frustration at good things not coming quite quickly enough!

Allergic to training?
Dogs can often damn-it sneeze when learning something new – they are excited by the potential for a reward, but a little frustrated because they aren't quite clear on how to earn it yet.

Achoo!

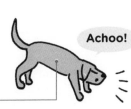

THE WHOLE DOG

To truly understand dog body language, you need to look at the whole picture.

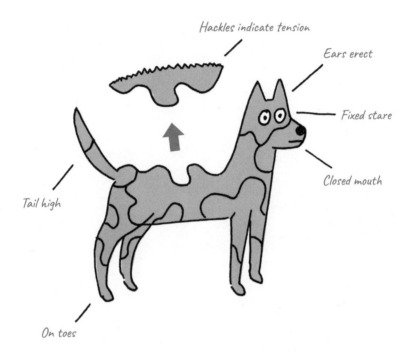

Hackles indicate tension

Ears erect

Fixed stare

Closed mouth

Tail high

On toes

PUT THE PIECES TOGETHER

Understanding dog body language is like completing a jigsaw puzzle – you need to put all the pieces together before you're able to see the full picture. A panting mouth might mean a dog is stressed, or it might simply mean the dog is hot – you won't know until you bring their ears, tail and stance into the mix, too. Eyes and ears full steam ahead and tail held high? This could be intense interest in something they want to chase, or they might be worried about what's ahead and ready to act... If the hair at their shoulders is spiky that might be the cue you need to tell you they're worried.

1
High or low?

The height of a dog's stance tells a story. Your dog standing tall on their toes with their head high is telling you they feel confident or alert. If they lower their head and body, they are indicating fear or a lack of confidence.

Roll over
Some relaxed dogs will roll over for a tummy scratch, but stressed dogs may also roll over as the ultimate form of body-lowering, indicating that they really mean no harm, or they are very scared.

2
Hackles

If you see the hair between your dog's shoulders rise, it's probably because they are feeling under threat. It's the same response you might have if you get goosebumps watching a scary movie.

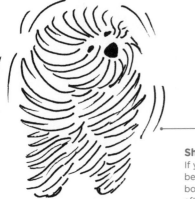

Shake off that stress
If you see your dog shake-off (as if they've been wet), this can be a sign of relief. It's the body-language equivalent of saying 'Phew!' after a tense moment passes.

3
Play bow

Happy face, elbows on the ground, paws out wide, bum up? That's a play bow!

'You up for a bit of fun?'
A play bow is normally saying 'Wanna play? Let's go!'

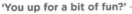

THE MEANING OF WOOF!

Your dog can be very vocal at times – barking, growling, howling and whining. What does all that doggy chat mean?

Woof! Woof!

THE BARK

Think of your dog's bark as a shout that could mean any number of things: an excited whoop; a 'get-off-my-property' threat; or a frustrated 'Come on Mum, throw that ball!' The key to understanding your dog's bark is the context – what's going on, what they might want and how they might be feeling.

The actual sound is also a clue. A low-pitched, deep bark tends to show that a dog means business; a higher-pitched bark often means that they are feeling low in confidence or desperately wanting to engage socially. And the more barks in a row there are, the more worked up a dog is likely to be...

1
Growl

A guttural growl tends to be a warning to give a dog space. It's an important part of doggy communication that says 'Stop doing that or there'll be trouble.' A dog might use a growl when they are stressed about grooming and wanting it to stop, or when they don't want their food to be taken, or out of frustration at being held back from doing something exciting.

It's not all serious
Dogs often growl during play – for example, during an enthusiastic game of tug – and this is normally nothing to worry about. In these situations your dog is probably saying 'Ooh yeah, soooooo fun!'*

Grrrr, oh yeah! Grrrr...

* Be aware that some dogs who are motivated to guard resources could bite if you attempt to remove something important from them.

Whine! whine!

2
Whine

Usually a whine or a whimper says a dog is seeking something. They may want attention, food, to be let outside, or for you to come back.

Intensity matters
The frequency and intensity of a whine tends to indicate how important your dog's desire is to them. If they *really* want to leave the vet clinic, feel *very* worried when left alone, or get *super* excited about a walk, their whine will escalate... even to the point it metamorphoses into a bark or howl!

Contagious howls
Howls are contagious – the sound of other dogs or even people howling is hard for some dogs to resist!

3
Howl

Howling is often to do with social connection. Dogs frequently howl when they're not coping well with being alone, essentially saying 'Please come back!' Dogs may also use howls territorially to say 'I'm here – this is my area.'

SIGNS THAT YOUR DOG NEEDS HELP

Your dog does not want to experience fear or anxiety. Knowing your dog's stress signs can help you to help them!

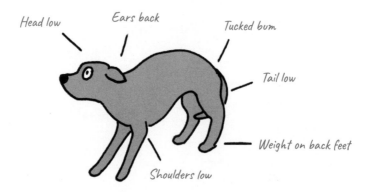

Head low   Ears back   Tucked bum

Tail low

Weight on back feet

Shoulders low

FEAR MAY COME IN A SHOUT – OR A WHISPER

Sometimes dogs are so clearly stressed they 'shout' it loudly enough that even us humans understand. A dog with a lowered head, body and tail, pinned ears and weight rearwards is clearly frightened.

However, are you aware of some of the more subtle signs your dog may be anxious or fearful? If you can identify when your dog is struggling to cope, you'll be better able to help them (see pages 142–9).

Furrowed brow

Ears rotated back

Turning head away,
and 'whale eye'

Trembling

Peeing at times they
should be able to hold on

Yawning

Lip-licking / lip-flicks

Panting – corners of
mouth pulled back

Jumpy and hypervigilant

Sweaty paw pads

Pacing

Slow movements
or freezing up

WHY DO DOGS DIG, EAT GRASS, CIRCLE, KICK THE GROUND?

Read on for answers to some of the burning mysteries of dog behaviour.

DIGGING

There are a number of reasons why your dog might attempt to relandscape your back yard.

- On a hot day, they might dig out a patch so they can benefit from the coolness of the deeper soil.

- They might be succumbing to an instinctual urge to seek and catch prey – especially in breeds like terriers, which have been selected to find and kill vermin.

- When a dog is stressed, they might dig to try to 'escape' the situation or simply defuse their stress (like us biting our nails).

- A pregnant dog sometimes 'nests' by digging out a den in a secluded spot before giving birth to her puppies.

- When an active dog is left in the garden with not much to do, digging can be their form of entertainment.

- If a dog has an important resource like a bone, or even a toy, they might bury it for later – much like the Vikings did to protect their loot!

1

Grass eating

Most dogs will eat grass at some point. Eating grass probably feels good for a dog. The question is: what benefit does it have? The answer is: we're not 100% sure!

Eat your greens

One of the most likely reasons dogs have evolved to enjoy eating grass is that it may provide beneficial nutrients and roughage. They might survive without greens, but a salad a day could keep the doctor away!*

* But double check with your vet that eating grass is safe for your particular dog, and ensure they are not eating grass sprayed with chemicals.

Old habits die hard

Your pampered pooch may not really need to primp their luxury dog bed with circling, but their inner wild dog can't help themselves!

2

Circling before lying down

Dogs often circle a few times before settling into their bed. This is probably an instinctual nesting behaviour from the days when their ancestors slept outdoors. It's the doggy equivalent of plumping their pillow.

3

Kicking the ground after toileting

When your dog enthusiastically kicks back grass and soil (called 'scraping') after toileting, this is not to cover their mess – it's actually marking behaviour. They're leaving a sign to other dogs, 'I was here, this is me!'

3D graffiti

When a dog scrapes, they are leaving multi-faceted canine graffiti – there's the visual mark left on the ground, the scent left from glands on a dog's feet, the scent of the urine or poo itself, and the real-time visual display of the kicking. Dogs really know how to leave their mark!

AND WHY DO THEY LICK ME, EAT POO, LIFT THEIR LEG, SCOOT?

More pressing questions answered!

FACE-LICKING

Doggy mums can regurgitate food for their pups to help them transition from milk to solids – and puppies lick their mum's lips to trigger this maternal takeaway order. Solicitous licking can extend into a dog's interactions with us when they want something. Don't worry, if your dog licks you, they don't want you to vomit. They may be asking for attention, dinner, play or a walk. Sometimes licking might also be a form of appeasement – indicating 'I don't mean any harm, glorious human.'*

---

* While being licked by a dog is usually fine for healthy people, there are certain circumstances when it's best avoided (see page 21).

1

Eating poo

As disgusting as it seems to us, coprophagia (eating poo) may just be a dog going back for seconds after the first pass through their digestive system – or that of another dog, or a cat or other animal!

Parasite protection

Coprophagia could be inherited from our dogs' wild ancestors. Many types of parasitic ova (eggs) that lurk in poo are not a problem initially, as they take around two days to develop into infective larvae. By eating the poo before the eggs develop into larvae, a dog may be trying to protect themselves and their family from future parasitic infections. It's a bit like using hand sanitiser to kill germs before they become a problem.

Parasite protected!

2

Lifting a leg to pee

In canine circles, urine is an important social signal. It communicates 'I was here, this is me.' Male dogs, especially uncastrated males, may lift their leg to ensure their urine mark is deposited more precisely and prominently on a bush, lamppost or Granny's handbag...

Female leg lifters

Female dogs can also lift one or even *both* rear legs to urine mark. It is thought that if a female dog is surrounded by brothers in the uterus before birth, she might absorb testosterone from them, and be more likely to display male-like behaviours such as leg-lifting later in life.

3

Scooting their bum on the ground

This behaviour tends to be linked with itchiness or discomfort – how else are they meant to scratch down there?!

Get to the bottom of the problem

Scooting could be a result of anal gland issues, parasites, or skin irritation owing to allergies or grooming rashes. If your dog is scooting, visit your vet to get to the bottom of the matter!

CHAPTER 4

HEALTH AND SAFETY

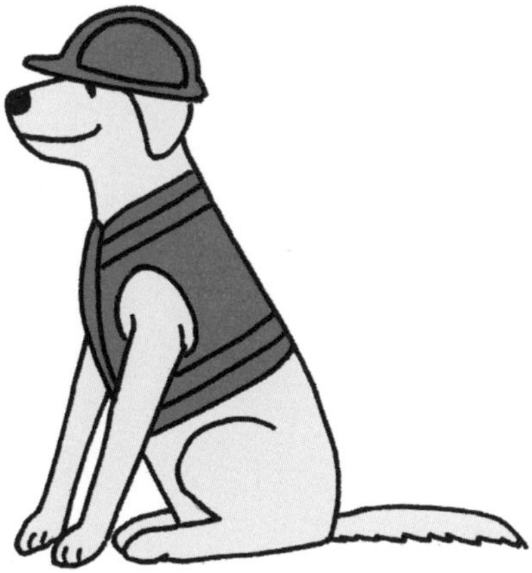

FEEDING

Good nutrition really makes a difference to your dog's health.

BALANCING YOUR DOG'S NUTRITIONAL NEEDS

There is much discussion around the best diets for dogs, but regardless of whether you feed store-bought or home-made, cooked or raw, wet food or kibble, meaty or vegetarian, the most important thing is to make sure the meal you give is nutritionally balanced – for your dog.

Dogs have different nutritional requirements from humans, and a badly balanced diet could negatively impact their health. Good signs that your dog is doing well on the diet you're feeding are a soft, glossy coat; smooth, elastic skin; and slightly soft, chocolate-brown, log-shaped poo.

1

Measure food

One of the most important things you can do for your dog's health is help them maintain a healthy weight. Often this is as simple as weighing out their food each day to ensure they don't receive too many calories. Reducing extras – like those crusts of buttery toast – also helps!

Fido's fabulous figure
Where on the spectrum is your dog?

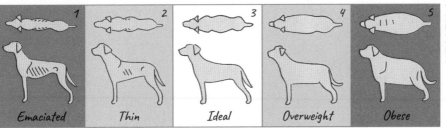

1	2	3	4	5
Emaciated	Thin	Ideal	Overweight	Obese

Special diets

Some foods are formulated specifically for animals with special requirements – for example, kidney problems, dental problems, food allergies or cognitive decline, or even just for those who need low-calorie food to help with weight loss.

2

Know their ideal weight

Having a number to aim for with your dog's weight can help keep you on track. If you have a smaller dog, an easy way to weigh them is to hold them while you stand on bathroom scales, then to subtract your own weight. For larger dogs, vet surgeries often have dog scales available to use free of charge.

More for Mum
A nursing mother should be given all the food she would like to eat – a tangle of puppies requires a lot of energy!

3

Changing needs

Puppies, adults and older dogs each require different things from their diet. Your energetic teenage pup or your sedate older dog with a few missing teeth will benefit from diets tailored to meet their specific nutritional, calorific and mechanical needs.

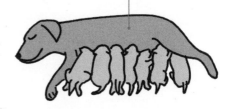

GROOMING IS MORE THAN JUST GLAMOUR!

Regular grooming isn't only for long-haired dogs – it's a key part of maintaining every dog's health.

Aha! Time for flea treatment, Gloria!

LOOKING AND FEELING GREAT

Grooming your dog is not only important for keeping them looking swish and ready for their next photo op, it's also a great time to run your hands and eyes over them to ensure they're healthy. By brushing, you'll ensure tangles don't get out of control and cause irritation or become unhygienic, and you'll also remove dirt, debris and dead skin.

As well as looking good, your dog is likely to feel better if you brush them regularly.

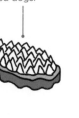

1

Brush type

Dog brushes come in many shapes and sizes – which one might be right for your dog?

Slicker brush: Excellent for removing matted hair on medium- to long-haired dogs.

Rubber brush: Accepted and often enjoyed by many dogs, and most effective with short-haired dogs.

Bristle brush: Works well with short-haired dogs to remove loose hair and debris.

Rake: Good for penetrating a thick coat and removing dead undercoat.

2

Brushing frequency

How often you brush your dog will depend on their coat. Smooth-haired dogs (like whippets or dalmatians) might need only a fortnightly rub-down with a rubber brush to remove loose hair and dead skin. Short-haired dogs with a dense undercoat (like retrievers) need a weekly brush. Dogs with long hair need brushing even more often.

Prevention is better than a cure

Dogs with curly or wavy coats (like poodle-crosses and bichon frise) or long, silky coats (like a Yorkshire terrier) may require daily brushing to keep matted hair at bay. You want to teach your dog that grooming is normal, painless and linked with a treat or two, rather than trying to deal with tangles once they've got out of control.

3

Parasite check

Brushing your dog is a great time to check for parasites such as ticks or fleas. If you see tiny black specks that look like pepper, this 'flea dirt' is a sign of undesirable hitchhikers! Take your dog (and their pesky hangers-on) to the vet for a parasite purge.

If you find a tick on your dog, a quick and easy way to remove it is with a Tick Twister, which also reduces the chance that the beastie's mouthparts will be left behind in your dog's skin.

TOOTH CARE

Good oral health can really improve the quality of your dog's life.

BRUSHING

Tooth care can be easy to overlook, but brushing your dog's teeth is one of the best ways to reduce dental problems in later life (imagine if you didn't brush your teeth for years – ewww!). If you're not able to brush your dog's choppers twice a day, brushing every other day will still do wonders and potentially save you a lot of money in vet bills further down the line.

Find a toothbrush designed for dogs, with soft bristles – this helps ensure the brushing is effective, while being as comfortable as possible for your dog. You will also need to use toothpaste designed for dogs, as some chemicals in human toothpaste aren't good for them. Some dog toothpastes come in flavours, like chicken, which your dog might enjoy. Yum!

1

Know the signs

Knowing the signs of tooth problems can really help your dog – no dog wants toothache! Watch for red and swollen gums, and excessive yellow or brown tartar build-up on the teeth.

Speed bumps
If your dog becomes slow or reluctant to eat, this could be a sign of dental issues.

Breath test
Let's face it, your dog's breath is never going to smell like roses, but if their breath really pongs, this might point to tooth troubles.

2

Chew it over

Providing chews that your dog enjoys gnawing on can really help to reduce the amount of plaque on their teeth.

3

How to make toothcare fun

Turn brushing from a chore into a fun routine. Brush your dog's teeth for just a few seconds, then, as the brush is touching their teeth or gums, say 'Yes!', stop brushing, and reach for a small food treat. Repeat this easy and rewarding routine ten times, then stop. That's the session done.

Get professional help
If the toothcare routine has slipped and your dog is looking more like Gollum than George Clooney, a visit to the vet for a professional clean will sharpen up that smile.

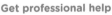

LEARNING TO LOVE THE VET

Teach your dog to love the vet so they can receive the medical care they need, with minimal stress and drama.

MAKE A SOCIAL VISIT!

Because visits to the clinic often occur when your dog is unwell or injured, the experience can be nerve-racking or even painful for your dog, and they might start to link the clinic with bad times. So, pop in for regular social visits, where nothing stressful or uncomfortable happens, and your dog gets plenty of small super-treats from both you and the staff. The clinic then becomes a party place, rather than a danger zone!

1

Which times are best for a visit?

Have a chat with the clinic to find times that work for social visits. If you make a plan, you'll be more likely to see it through.

It's in the diary!
Incorporate fun visits to the clinic into your dog's schedule. You might plan a weekly trip to a park that is near your vet, and drop in on the way.

Food treats at clinic!

Handling hand-outs
Something that can help many dogs is spending time on an examination table, receiving regular small treats from you while they are gently stroked by one of the vet team.

2

Build positive links

When you make your social visits, don't simply pop a wet nose around the door and then go. Walk in together and ask the staff to give your dog a good scratch behind the ears and a treat – that way your dog will start to associate being handled by the vet with the good stuff!

Chill pill
If your dog requires medical attention and you aren't yet at the point where they can cope emotionally with the procedure, your vet might give your Nervous Nelly anti-anxiety medication. That can help prevent one visit causing set-backs to your dog's confidence.

3

Balancing act

Keep building your dog's confidence at the clinic by having the nurses do simple checks like looking in their ears or mouth, but be ready to ease off if your dog becomes fearful (see pages 88–9 for how to read the signs that your dog may have had enough).

WARNING SIGNS OF ILLNESS

Your dog can't tell you with words that they're feeling under the weather, so it's important to be aware of signs that might indicate illness.

WATCH FOR BEHAVIOUR CHANGES

One of the most important signs of ill health is a change in your dog's behaviour. You know your dog, and that means you're the one in the best position to notice!

If they become withdrawn or lethargic, or they're sleeping more than usual, it could mean they're not well. Restlessness, irritability or aggression can also indicate illness. Yelping, limping, stiffness and a reluctance to engage in normal activities should ring warning bells, too. Call your vet clinic to book a health check, especially if you also notice any of the signs on the opposite page.

Loss of appetite

Eating less, or refusing food, especially for more than 24 hours.

Weight loss

Loss of weight over a period of days or weeks with no obvious explanation.

Respiratory changes

Coughing, sneezing, wheezing, laboured breathing, discharge from nose.

Thirst

Drinking much more water than usual – or losing interest in it.

Tummy troubles

Vomiting or diarrhoea.

Excessive peeing

Urinating more frequently.

Eye changes

Dry, red or cloudy eyes, or discharge.

Head movements

Head-shaking or holding their head at an angle.

Skin

Dry, flaky, itchy skin. Skin that's red rather than pink. Lumps or sores.

Fur

Dry, dull fur that feels rough and brittle. Excessive shedding, or bald patches.

COMMON HEALTH PROBLEMS

Here are some of the most common doggy health problems that veterinarians see day in, day out.

THE BIG SIX

Having an insight into the six most common issues that vets come across will help you identify them early to nip them in the bud, or even prevent them occurring altogether. Your dog needs a health mentor!

Make sure you also look after other basics, like parasite control. Internal parasites (such as tapeworms, roundworms, whipworms, hookworms and lungworms) and external parasites (like fleas, ticks and mites) can cause big problems for your pooch. Administering parasite treatment is an easy, cheap and effective way to keep your dog healthy, happy and raring to go!

1st: Gum disease (12.5%)*

Sitting at the top of the list is gum disease, accounting for one in eight trips to the vet. Plaque builds on teeth and hardens into tartar, which over time can cause big problems for a dog's teeth and gums. The good news is there are ways to protect your dog from dental dodginess (see pages 100–101).

* O'Neill, D.G., James, H., Brodbelt, D.C. et al. Prevalence of commonly diagnosed disorders in UK dogs under primary veterinary care: results and applications. BMC Vet Res 17, 69 (2021)

2nd: Ear infections (7.3%)

Ear infections come second. Often caused by bacteria or yeast thriving in the moist warm conditions of the ear, they can be very painful for your dog, and should be seen to quickly.

3rd: Obesity (7.1%)

Unfortunately, Bruce may not be 'big boned' – he needs to lose a few pounds to avoid the third-most common health issue for dogs: obesity-related problems.

4th: Overgrown nails (5.5%)

Dogs' nails need to be worn down through adequate exercise, or clipped, to prevent them splitting, tearing or breaking, which can be very painful. Long nails can also put uneven stress on parts of a dog's foot and cause lameness – a bit like humans wearing high-heels every day!

5th: Anal sac issues (4.8%)

Did you know that dogs have two special glands on their bottom that release social scents that are informative to other dogs? These can sometimes become blocked, infected and painful – watch for scooting (see page 93)!

6th: Diarrhoea (3.8%)

It's amazing what some dogs will eat if they get a chance (yes, we're looking at you, Bruce!), so it's no wonder they get diarrhoea at times. Sometimes loose poo can indicate more serious issues, though.

NEUTERING MALE DOGS

Removal of a dog's 'crown jewels' is a decision that we need to make for the right reasons – after all, once they're gone, they're gone. Discuss neutering (and its timing) with your vet to ensure it's the right decision for your boy.

WILL NEUTERING CALM MY DOG DOWN?

Without his testicles, a dog no longer produces the hormone testosterone, which contributes to masculine behaviours. For example, a castrated dog is less likely to be found urine marking, strutting the streets looking for romantic liaisons, indulging in questionable sexual behaviour, and engaging in biffo with other males. However, it's wrong to assume that neutered males will necessarily be *calmer*, because (contrary to popular belief) testosterone doesn't tend to make dogs excitable or unruly.

1

Testosterone and aggression

Testosterone can mean a dog is quicker to react aggressively, and can make the hostility more intense and longer lasting. Therefore, males who are entire can be more likely than neutered dogs to lash out in challenging situations. Many dogs behave less aggressively once testosterone levels drop after castration.

Neutering nervousness

Be aware that testosterone can act as a confidence booster, so in some cases the lack of testosterone after castration may mean a dog becomes more sensitive emotionally and therefore – perhaps surprisingly to a human – more likely to react aggressively when feeling under threat.

No quick fix

Even if testosterone is influencing an unwanted behaviour, castration may not be the easy fix many hope that it will be.

2

The bigger picture

While testosterone can influence some types of unwanted behaviour, there are normally other factors at play, too – such as a dog's environment, prior learning, individual personality, and brain-wiring before birth and during puberty.

3

Who ate all the pies?

Neutering will not make your dog put on the pounds – as long as you help them keep active and don't overfeed them.

Unplanned puppies

By neutering your dog, you are doing your part to reduce unplanned litters, and the number of unwanted dogs in the world.

SPAYING FEMALE DOGS

Unless you're committed to breeding responsibly, and all the hard work that goes into it, spaying is the best way to avoid the twice-yearly challenge of your gorgeous girl being in heat.

WILL SPAYING IMPROVE HER BEHAVIOUR?

Spaying a female dog removes her ovaries, which are responsible for reproductive hormones such as oestrogen and progesterone. As a result, spaying can help improve problem behaviours that occur around the time a female is in season. For example, if a female experiences false pregnancies, guards her toys as if they were her babies, and is protective of her bed, spaying may help resolve these misplaced maternal urges.

Spaying is unlikely to improve or worsen unwanted behaviour that is not linked to her oestrous cycle.

1

Mind the mess

Female dogs who have not been spayed drip blood when they are in season. Cleaning up hardwood floors might just be a bit of a hassle, but a cream carpet – forget it!

Girlie britches
It's possible to use special doggy underwear to minimise the cleaning-up required with a female in heat, but not all dogs are convinced of their merits!

2

Health pros and cons

There are health benefits and risks involved with spaying. Speak to your vet to ensure spaying (and the age at which it is done) is the right choice for your individual pet.

One size does not fit all
Large breeds may benefit from delaying their spaying a little longer than small breeds.

3

Spaying and nervousness

Hormonal changes from spaying will not make your dog more nervous, but a stressful experience at the vet clinic might. As always, ensure time at the vet clinic is as low stress as possible before and after the procedure.

Pffft! It's for my own good.

Recovery time
After your girl has been spayed, you may need to restrict her activity for ten days or so. Also, so she doesn't lick and damage her wound site, your vet might recommend a 'cone of shame'...

FOODS TO AVOID

Some dogs will eat pretty much whatever they can lay their paws on, but they don't always know what's good for them!

PHYSICAL DANGERS

Some everyday foods can be toxic for dogs, while others present injury risks.

Cooked bones are often brittle and may splinter, which can block or even puncture a dog's stomach. Innocent-looking corn on the cob doesn't tend to break down in a dog's stomach so can also cause blockages – especially when a greedy-guts swallows a cob whole! Even harmless-looking bread dough may be a problem, as it can swell up in the warm, moist tummy of a dog.*

---

* These aren't the only foods a dog should avoid eating – ask your vet for comprehensive advice before feeding your dog anything not specifically intended for doggy dinner.

1
Chocolate

Given half a chance, many dogs will wolf down a mislaid bar of chocolate, but theobromine, a compound in chocolate, is poisonous for them.

Dangers in the dark
Dark chocolate and baking chocolate contain the most theobromine, so are the riskiest.

Not for you, Trixie!

2
Grapes

Some dogs seem to be able to eat grapes with no ill effects, while others can experience stomach issues and even life-threatening kidney failure. Keep your dog safe by ensuring grapes, currants and sultanas stay firmly on the forbidden list.

Raisins
Raisins are of course dried grapes, and are in many foods like biscuits, cereal and bread. Watch for hidden raisins if you're considering giving your dog a snack meant for humans!

3
Xylitol

The artificial sweetener xylitol is in many human foods, but even small amounts can cause a spike in insulin in dogs, and plummeting blood-sugar levels. Eaten in higher quantities, it can cause liver failure. This is one food additive you need to keep an eye out for – and give a wide berth.

Foods to check
Any food that has been sweetened could contain xylitol – chewing gum, sugar-free sweets, sugar alternatives and diet foods are common sources. Also, watch out for substances such as toothpaste, cough drops, and chewable vitamins – we all know dogs who will give anything a taste!

ROAD TRIP!

Keep your dog safe when hitting the highway.

SAFETY FIRST

For many dogs there's nothing better in life than a road trip. The possibilities a car unlocks are endless – the park, beach, forest, river, or their best friend's house are all just a ride away! You must get everyone there safely though, so you need to restrain your dog appropriately, as well as keep them cool and protect them from hazards.

1

Why restrain your dog in the car?

Keeping your dog under control while you're driving is important for two reasons: 1) it prevents them from distracting you as you drive and 2) in the event of a crash, both you and your dog will be better protected.

Boot barrier
Cars aren't designed with dog safety in mind, so it can be hard to find the perfect safety solution. A fitted dog-guard designed specifically for your car model that bolts to secure points in the car will keep your dog safely in the boot while giving them plenty of room to lie down. Added bonus – it will also stop them from drooling on any passengers in the back seat!

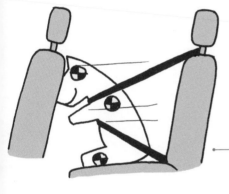

Crash tested
Most harnesses aren't strong enough to safely restrain your dog in an accident. If you go for the harness option, choose one that has undergone crash testing.

2

Using a harness

Never use your dog's collar to secure them in the car. In an accident the collar would transfer dangerous forces to their neck. Instead, you can use a special harness that attaches to the seatbelt to keep your dog safe.

Window safety
Many dogs will put their head out of an open window to soak in the wonderous smells, but flying insects can injure their eyes, and there's a risk they might jump out. Lower the window just enough that they can sample the delicious turbo-charged smells, without risk to life and limb.

3

Hot cars

Dogs can't cool themselves in the same way humans can, and can overheat very quickly in a hot car. Never leave a dog unattended in a car.

PUT UP A FENCE

Securely enclosing your dog's precious outdoor space at home keeps them safe, and is peace of mind for you.

SECURE THE PERIMETER!

Your home's outdoor space is a valuable resource for your dog, providing wonderful opportunities like sun-bathing, air-scenting, and racing and wrestling with a housemate, or foraging for their lunch (see page 127). However, you need to be confident they are not able to get out and risk injury on roads, cause trouble with other dogs or people, chase animals, or consummate the forbidden romance with the girl next door. You need to be able to trust in your fencing, so you can relax in the knowledge that you have Houdini contained!

1
How high?

I think this will be a new personal best.

The height of fence you need depends on your dog's size, athleticism, climbing skill and motivation to escape. A good general rule is to have a fence three times higher than your dog is at the shoulder. But, some dogs will conquer even that fence easily and you will need to go higher.

Start tall
Aim to do your fencing once, and do it properly. If you start low and add height because your dog proves they're able to escape, you risk training them to become an expert jumper or climber. Escapee success breeds success, so start tall!

Determined diggers
For tunnelling types, add an L-shaped length of mesh on the ground along your fence.

3
Types of fence

Two common types of fence are 'solid-barrier' and 'chain-link'. Solid barrier fences are excellent deterrents as they tend to be secure and they block your dog from seeing enticing things on the other side (and they look good, too). Chain-link fences are quick to erect and cost-effective, but some dogs can climb them. Plus, with full visuals on the world outside, your dog may have an irresistible temptation to explore.

Latches
To make the most of your gloriously impenetrable dog fence, make sure you can easily and securely close the gate. A little extra money on a good latch is worth its weight in gold.

2
Beefing up security

Some dogs require the Alcatraz treatment. If your dog is jumping or climbing over your fence, consider adding extra height but angled inwards at 45 degrees. For the most dedicated escapee, consider adding a rolling top to the fence to prevent a paw-hold.

CHAPTER

5

MAXIMUM HAPPINESS

HOME COMFORTS

A dog's home is their castle. Here are some key ideas to make your dog feel like a king or queen!

SOCIAL CONTACT

Most dogs are extroverts and want social contact. Set up your house so they can be part of the human action if they want, but also provide quiet places for your dog to go if life gets too hectic – especially if there are young children around. Establish a rule with the family that your dog is not to be disturbed when they go to their retreat space for a little 'me-time'.

Being at home by themselves for long periods can be tough for your pooch, or at least very boring. If you are all going to be out for the day, consider doggy day-care, or drop your dog off with a friend who also has a dog, or ask your dog-mad neighbour to pop in to 'adopt' them for the afternoon.

1
The water bowl

Your dog needs access to plenty of fresh, clean water. If you see them drinking out of the toilet, they are probably trying to tell you there's a problem with their hydration set-up! To help put things right, empty and replace your dog's water at least once a day.

What makes a good water bowl?
Stainless steel bowls with rubber feet work well, as they are easy to clean, hygienic, non-toxic and unlikely to break. And your dog is less likely to chew them!

2
The bed

It's no wonder dogs like to steal our spot on the sofa. Often the beds we provide for them are decidedly second-rate! Choose one that is large enough for them to lie on with their legs stretched out to the side, deep enough to cope with their weight, and has raised edges so they can snuggle up without the indignity of slipping off on to the floor.

A little luxury
Many dogs, especially older dogs who might be feeling the aches and pains of later life, will appreciate a memory-foam inner.

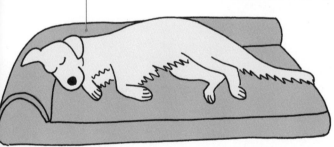

Super-charge the tech
Some remote monitoring devices allow you to speak to your dog, and even deliver rewards!

3
Remote dog monitor

Consider getting a dog-cam to monitor your dog while you're out. When you review the footage, you might notice events that worry them and then you can make reassuring adjustments. You'll also see what your dog enjoys doing most when they're home alone!

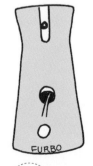

DO DOGS LIKE HUGS?

Do our dogs enjoy cuddles and kisses? Or are these mainly for our benefit? There's no simple answer to this – it depends very much on the dog and how we approach snuggling up.

DIFFERENT STROKES FOR DIFFERENT FOLKS

We always want to show our dogs just how much we love them, and we tend to do this in ways that come naturally to us – with hugs and kisses. Some dogs find it extremely nerve-racking when humans get face-to-face with them, especially if they're restrained in a 'hug'. Others aren't too bothered and will tolerate our strange invasions of their personal space, and some genuinely seem to love every second of in-your-face smooching.

1

Consent is crucial

The key to figuring out if your dog is okay with your affection is to do a *consent test*. Give them the chance to turn away or move off... if they do, they're probably not enjoying it! Try instead to show your love for them in ways they will enjoy (see below).

Here we go again
A firm pat on a dog's head is the equivalent of Great Aunt Beatrice pinching you on the cheek because 'you're so cute'.

Signs of delight
You'll know when you're hitting just the right spot with a massage when your dog's eye-lids become droopy and they lean right into your hand.

2

Doing it right

Most dogs love physical contact if it's done in the right way. Let them cuddle into you rather than restraining them with a hug, while you massage their cheeks, neck, chest and back, and behind the ears.

Kissing us back
If we hug or kiss a dog and they lick us, it's natural to think they are kissing us back. With some dogs licking can indeed be a happy, greeting behaviour, but with others it might be a stressed attempt to appease the 'threat' of the interaction.

3

Kids and hugging

Children are particularly keen to hug, kiss and cuddle dogs, so help them understand how to respect your dog's (and other dogs') social boundaries. Watch for signs of stress like 'whale eye' (see page 89), and step in to help give your dog the space they need. It's critical kids know not to attempt cuddles with unfamiliar dogs, who can sometimes get scared and bite defensively.

THE LOVE OF EXERCISE

Exercise is an essential part of a dog's overall wellbeing – and yours!

THERE'S MORE TO A WALK THAN EXERCISE

Daily walks with your dog are about more than just the physical exercise (although, of course, that's important). A walk is an opportunity for your dog to explore the big wide world away from the familiarity of home. Soaking in scents, interacting with other dogs and people, having new experiences, and spending quality time with you are all reasons why walks are so valuable for your dog. We all need to get away from the house sometimes, and for a dog this should be at least once a day.

1

Better behaviour

It's often said that a tired dog is a happy, well-behaved dog. Dogs with lots of energy and no opportunity to run, sniff and play will be more likely to engage in unwanted behaviour at home, so make sure your pooch gets out and about regularly.

Pets with benefits

Researchers have found that dog owners are four times more likely to get enough exercise compared to non-dog owners – your dog is your partner in fitness!

How much and how often?

The ideal amount of exercise each day varies from at least 30 minutes for small breeds, to two or more hours for large and high-energy dogs who struggle to fulfil their get-up-and-go at home. It's even better if you can divide exercise time into a couple of sessions to spread out the action.

2

Keeping trim

Along with an appropriate diet, exercising your dog will help them maintain a healthy weight (see page 97). This is one of the best things you can do for your dog's health, and sets them up for a long and active life.

Gambolling around with a geriatric dog

Small, frequent bouts of play and exercise are a good way to keep your older dog healthy, and as fit as they're able to be. Even little bits of exercise around the house and garden can make a difference to an elderly dog – so don't feel duty bound to do a lap of the park if their body language tells you it's a bit much.

3

Age appropriate

While you might have a decades-long commitment to trail running or mountain biking, your dog may not be able to join you when they're a young puppy, or as an ageing or unwell dog. Be mindful of their capabilities, and remember to scale back activity if you notice they're struggling.

FOOD FUN

Make the most of your dog's daily food ration to engage
their brain throughout the day.

DITCH THE FOOD BOWL

Feeding your dog in a bowl is so last century! There are plenty of much more fun ways to feed.

Each morning, measure out your dog's food for the day, and put it aside (this works best for dry food). Then, whenever you get a chance, grab a handful of this daily allowance and use it to create or engage in a stimulating activity for your pooch. Your dog will have a ball – perhaps even a puzzle ball (like the ones opposite)!

1

Forage feeding

Sometimes the simplest ideas are the best. Scatter a portion of the day's food out on the lawn or garden, so your dog engages their scenting super-powers to hunt down their meal. The beauty of this activity is that they will never know if they've found the last piece, and often go back for a second, third or even fourth sweep just to make sure!

Have I found every piece?

Up the challenge

Once your dog becomes a pro with the forage-feeding routine, you can hide a few special 'dessert' pieces (pea-sized bits of cheese or frankfurter) in challenging places, like under a rock or above their head-height in a tree.

Start off easy

Your dog will need to build confidence with a puzzle feeder. Start simply: *almost* fill the feeder with food that has a little grated cheese mixed in – this will ensure your dog's motivation is high and the food falls out easily.*

2

Puzzle feeders

Add a handful of food to an interactive feeder like a puzzle ball or bottom-weighted wobbler. Your dog will need to roll or topple the feeder about to gradually free the kibble hostages inside!

3

Stuff a Kong

Stuff a rubber Kong toy with a delicious mixture of food. The resulting licking and gnawing will be a wonderful activity for your dog. By freezing this package of delight, you can prolong the fun.

101 ways to stuff a Kong*

Get imaginative with your Kong stuffing – your dog will love you for it. Who knows what their favourite recipe might be: is it banana, yogurt and peanut butter mixed with their dry food? Or maybe a little tuna, blueberry and egg...

* Check with your vet to ensure your ingredients are safe for your dog. For example, avoid blue cheese, make sure peanut butter doesn't contain xylitol (see page 113) and that your dog is tolerant to the lactose in yogurt.

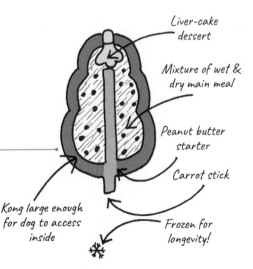

Liver-cake dessert

Mixture of wet & dry main meal

Peanut butter starter

Carrot stick

Kong large enough for dog to access inside

Frozen for longevity!

THE FIND-IT GAME

The 'find-it' game is an exciting and rewarding way to switch on your dog's brain and sense of smell.

TRAINING 'FIND-IT'

Teaching your dog how to play the 'find-it' game is easy. Ask someone to hold your dog's collar, show the dog you have an enticing morsel of food and move to the door of the room. Put the food on the floor and say 'Find it!' The other person should then release your dog to scamper towards the food to snuffle it up! Easy right? From here, try repeating the routine, but this time put the food just out of sight around the corner before saying 'Find it!' The next step is to move even further away so that you are out of sight before you place the food down. Then, return to your dog to say 'Find it!' Nice work – you're now on track for a first-class find-it.

1

Up the ante

As long as your dog keeps succeeding with their searching, you can slowly increase the challenge from 'just round the corner' to 'it could be anywhere'.

It's got to be somewhere...

MAXIMUM HAPPINESS

Seek and you shall find
When you play advanced-level 'find-it', the super-treat treasure could be any location where your dog is permitted access. It might be behind the sofa, or perched halfway up your back fence. Your canine chum will know just one thing for certain – if they seek, they shall find!

Stay...

2

Practising 'stay'

Double up your training by using the 'stay' routine (see pages 72–3) while you move out of sight to hide the goodies.

But don't get ahead of yourself
Make sure your dog is good enough at 'stay' before you try this out! You'll need to disappear out of sight for a minute...

3

Toy hunting

A fun variation is to hide one of your dog's favourite toys, and then send them to find it. Dogs love the excitement of searching for their toy, and the additional thrill of a game of tug or fetch once they proudly bring it back to you.

Super searchers
If you're really ready to take it to the next level, train your dog to recognise the name of *different* toys. The key is to make sure you reward them only with play or food if they bring back the toy you've asked for. One very impressive dog has memorised more than 1,000 different toy names – could you and your dog eventually break the world record?

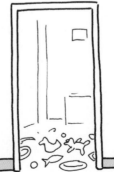

Find Ducky!

THE TUG GAME

Make the most of your dog's desire to play tug – it's a wonderful game!

WHAT A GAME!

A game of tug offers physical exercise and a very enjoyable social interaction between you and your dog. Importantly, though, it will also help teach them to listen at times of high excitement. All in all, a game of tug is an *amaaaazing* bit of quality time for the two of you!

1

Tug done right

Provide your dog with a tug toy that looks and feels different from things you don't want them to grab and shake (for example, rope toys are good, old shoes less so). Encourage your dog to grab the toy, hold, pull, shake and generally have rip-roaring fun!

GRRRRR

Will it make my dog aggressive?
There is a myth that tug games will make your dog aggressive. While some dogs can compete aggressively over toys, if your dog is having fun with a tug game, the growly thrill of this play is unlikely to turn a peaceful personality into a savage!

Doggy Zen
By teaching your dog to control their excitement, and to give up their fun in order to restart it, each game of tug will be an important lesson in self-control for them.

2

Drop to restart

In the middle of tugging craziness, calmly say 'drop', and bring the toy against your leg so it is dead and boring. Then wait. And wait some more. Your dog might keep holding and pulling, but it won't be much fun. Then... once they finally *voluntarily* let go, say 'Yes!' and immediately push the toy *towards* them and start the exuberant tug game again.

If you love something, let it go.

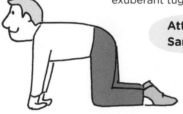

Attaboy Sammy!

3

Expect more

Once your dog has the hang of the release-to-restart idea, you can increase the challenge: wait for them to back off further from the toy or ask them to sit before you restart the fun.

Give them a win
We all need a win sometimes and our dogs are no exception. If your dog gives a particularly strong shake during the tug game, you can pretend they've beaten you by letting go – just as long as it's not after you've asked them to drop!

WORK THAT NOSE!

You've got a good 'find-it' going (see pages 128–9), but it would be a pity to stop there. Here are three more scent games to help you work this canine super-power.

1
Which hand?

The Two-Hand Game is quick and easy fun. Allow your dog to see you have a tasty titbit, and transfer the food into one of your closed hands (don't let them see which one).

Now choose!
Hold both closed hands out to your dog, let them sniff, and wait for them to paw at a hand. Open the chosen hand. If it's empty, act very sad and do the treat shuffle again. If they've picked correctly, act very excited and let them take the treat!

2

The magic cup

Show your dog a morsel of food, then place it under a plastic cup. When your dog nudges the cup with their nose or paw, say 'Wow!' and lift the cup to let them take the food. Some dogs might bowl the cup over straight away, which is also allowed.

One cup, two cup, three cup, more!
Once your dog understands this game, introduce two, three or even four cups. Place the food under one, then slide the cups around to different positions so your dog needs to sniff out which cup the treat is under. Repeat until the fun wears off for you or your dog – just be aware that if you have a Labrador, this might be five hours later!

3

Track back

This game is gold. Take a favourite small toy – a ball, a teddy or a rope-toy – with you on a walk. Once you're walking through open space and your dog is concentrating on other things, drop the toy! Walk on a few steps, call your dog, and excitedly encourage them to find it (using a prompt such as 'Seek' or 'Where's your ball?'). When your dog finds it, reward them with a treat or play a game with the toy.

Make the scent trail longer
Once your dog understands that finding the toy pays handsomely, start to walk further after dropping it. Your dog now needs to start following the scent of your footsteps back to where you let go of the toy. How far can you get your dog tracking back to find their beloved treasure?

Where's your ball?

MAKE A DIG-PIT

Let's build a dig-pit for your dog, so your lawn, garden and prize roses don't suffer from their digging desires!

Trust me Loki, this spot is much better.

I DIG IT!

Let's face it, dogs love a good digging session (see page 90). Rather than leaving it up to them to decide which part of the garden is the best digging target, you can provide them with a dedicated dig-pit that they can excavate to their heart's content! Not only will this targeted intervention save your garden, but it will also provide your dog with a wonderful action station right in your back yard.

1

Build it and they will come

Your dog's new dig-pit should have well-defined boundaries, made from something like untreated wooden 'sleepers'. This has two benefits – it helps hold in a good amount of dirt or sand, and clearly shows your dog where they can dig.

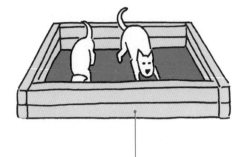

Go big

A good size for your dog's dig-pit is 2 metres long by 1 metre wide and 50cm deep. In terms of sleepers, that's likely to be one sleeper long, and half a sleeper wide.

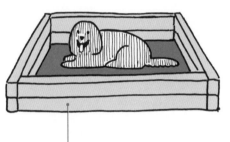

2

Fill the dig-pit

Sand is a good material to fill the pit with, as your dog can shake off the grains after their session, rather than coming back inside covered in dirt!

Moisture is cool

Wetting the sand regularly can make digging even better fun for your dog, as the grains will clump together more. A moist pit also really helps if your dog is digging for a cool place to lie down.

3

Buried treasure

Once the dig-pit is set up, you can bury food, chew-toys or other goodies in it. In the early days, show your dog you are burying something and even join them in digging it out. You want them to learn that the dig-pit is a goldmine compared to other garden locations!

Surprise finds

When your dog isn't looking, bury amazing finds like a frozen, food-stuffed Kong toy for them to uncover (see page 127 for 'recipes'). Start with shallow burying, but as your dog becomes more committed to treasure hunting, bury the rewards deeper and deeper. In your dog's mind, the dig-pit will become a location of magically refilling digging delight!

CHAPTER

6

HOUSTON, WE HAVE A PROBLEM

JUMPING UP

Does your dog jump up at people despite all your efforts to persuade them not to? How rude! Here's how you can teach them some polite new manners.

WHY DOGS JUMP UP

Dogs jump up because they want attention. They're excited to see us, and want desperately to give and receive love.

A dog's jumping-up habit often starts young, as puppies learn through sheer power of cuteness that if they get two paws on someone, the doting will come. When they hit the gangly adolescent phase, this behaviour becomes less endearing, *but it still works*. They may continue to get the occasional cuddle, and jumping up might also get a response in other ways. For many dogs, any attention is better than no attention! When humans look at a dog, attempt to reassure them, give requests (such as 'Off!'), push them back to the ground, or even tell them off, it can all reinforce jumping up.

1

'But they know they shouldn't'

Often a dog will temporarily stop jumping up when we say 'Off' or we push them away. This isn't because they understand they aren't allowed to, it's because they've accomplished their mission – they've got attention!

Repeat performance
The pattern keeps repeating when a dog gets a reaction from us humans each time they jump up. We may imagine we're 'training' them to stop, but actually we've achieved the opposite...

This will stop her jumping up.

No! Off!

She spoke to me!

Please stroke him only when he has four feet on the floor.

2

Encouraging good manners

To break the jumping-up habit, the most important thing to do is to *take the initiative to interact with your dog when they are being polite, with four feet on the floor*. Don't wait for them to demand attention.

Meeting strangers
Keep your dog on a lead when you're around new people. This will give you a chance to explain the 'four-on-the-floor' rule, while preventing your bouncy dog from jumping up in the meantime.

3

Put on your poker face!

If your dog does jump up, completely ignore them. Cross your arms, turn away, don't look at them, and resist saying anything. (This strategy works for other attention-grabbing too, like barking.)

Frustration burst
At first, when you stop responding to them jumping up, your dog may do it even more – or they might try other 'look-at-me' strategies, like barking. Don't worry, once you get past this burst of frustration their kangaroo act will ease off.

PULLING ON THE LEAD

Does your dog steam ahead on walks, pulling you along on the lead? Here's how to take the strain out of your strolls.

WHY DOGS PULL

Leaving home for a walk is often the highlight of a dog's day, and they're enticed to chase all the fascinating smells and opportunities for fun – whether that's the scent of another dog, the chance to meet a passer-by, or the promise of off-lead thrills at the park around the corner.

From a young age many dogs learn that the best way to get to these wonderful things is to pull persistently and forcefully on their lead. For them, the reward of making progress outweighs any discomfort. If pulling pays off, it can easily become an ingrained habit!

1

What's the solution?

The key to successful 'loose-lead walking' is ensuring your dog doesn't ever make forward progress when they are pulling. Instead, allow them to get to interesting stuff *when the lead is loose and comfortable.*

Give a dog some slack

If you're having pulling troubles, it's tempting to use a very short lead, or rein a long one in tight. However, this can make the problem worse! Your dog will have little opportunity to learn the benefit of keeping the lead loose if it's tight all the time.

I'll have to drag the human with me.

2

A loose lead works

You want your dog to have the opportunity to learn that keeping slack in the lead will mean they get more chances to sniff out interesting doggy news (see page 15). So, relax and give them a little more freedom (as long as they keep the lead slack). Sniffing is what a walk is all about!

3

Pulling never pays

Be consistent in drawing a clear line for your dog with this simple technique: every single time they pull on a tight lead for more than three steps, immediately start walking backwards until they are walking towards you. Now you can both head in the original direction again. Pulling delays the good times!

Helping out

If you're happy for your dog to approach something, help them get there on a loose lead. Rather than having them pull you to that lamp post they're desperate to sniff, give them a little extra slack in the lead as you approach.

Helpful tools

A head collar or chest-attaching harness can do wonders if you use them with these training methods. Avoid a back-attaching harness though, as it can make pulling dogs worse – think Huskies pulling sleds! (See also page 49.)

WHAT IS FEAR?

Fear is an emotion that can help a dog stay safe in dangerous situations. It triggers their body's fight-or-flight response, so they're tuned-up for physical action.

FIGHT-OR-FLIGHT RESPONSE

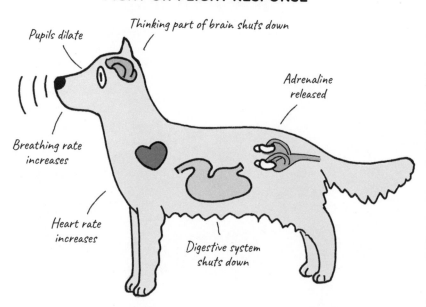

Pupils dilate

Thinking part of brain shuts down

Adrenaline released

Breathing rate increases

Heart rate increases

Digestive system shuts down

WHEN FEAR IS MISPLACED

Fear is natural and normal, but it's not always appropriate: some dogs can be worried about things they needn't be. Friendly stranger = danger! New dog = danger! Home alone for five minutes = danger! If you're wondering why your dog gets so unnecessarily stressed about some things, often the answer is that their genetics have wired up their brain this way, and/or their early experience may have been too limited (see pages 30–31). The good news is there are things you can do to help your sensitive dog grow in confidence.

Three golden rules for reducing fear

Fear can be irrational and powerful, and take over the thinking part of a dog's brain. As much as we'd like to stop our dogs *ever* feeling overwhelmed with fear, sometimes this just isn't possible. What you need to do is figure out what your dog is scared of and work to reduce their fear over time, using the three golden rules below.

1

Avoid overwhelming situations

Dropping your dog in at the deep end of scary doesn't help – if they're terrified of something, don't push it! Instead, help them to develop their confidence in less intense situations and build up from there.

Big frights don't help
If a dog gets a really big fright from something they're already nervous of, it can worsen their fear.

2

Spend time with the scary thing

Whatever your dog is scared of, help them spend time getting used to it, *in tolerable doses*. Always stick with a level of 'danger' they can cope with. If they show signs of stress (see pages 88–9) or refuse a food treat, reduce the intensity of the situation – or come back to it another day.

Slow and steady wins the race
Each minute your dog spends around things that scare them will slowly but surely reduce their fear.

3

Create a positive link

If a situation that seemed scary is linked with something wonderful, your dog will start to feel differently about it. Make sure the positive experience *follows* the challenge, though, to ensure that *scary thing brings happiness*, rather than good times becoming a signpost for fright!

Going forward with food
If you consistently share lots of little super-treats when your dog is in situations they find slightly nerve-racking, these situations will start to predict good times.

Treat!

I like it when spidey comes.

COPING WITH LOUD NOISES

It's common for sudden noises like fireworks, gunshots or thunder to frighten dogs. But, there are practical ways we can help them to cope with scary sounds.

HELP YOUR DOG COPE

If your dog is sound phobic, one of your most important jobs is to prevent them getting big frights. Avoid walking after dusk during firework season or if the weather looks thundery, as the risk of a random bang isn't worth the potential long-term effects for your dog. When you're at home and can't avoid scary noises (a loud celebration next door or a storm, say), set up the house so your dog is better able to cope. Observe where your dog naturally seeks refuge when they're scared, and build them a sound-sanctuary there. This could be an open dog-crate covered in thick blankets to muffle the sounds, with blankets on the floor where they can 'dig' to alleviate stress.

You may not be able to turn off the fireworks, but with strategies like this, you can help to 'turn them down' for your dog.

1

Anti-anxiety medication

Some dogs get so stressed by sounds, it's necessary to help them through specific, overwhelming events with anti-anxiety medication from a vet. This will reduce the stress of the experience for them, and stop their phobia worsening over time.

It's OK to comfort your dog!
Some people are concerned that comforting their dog when they're scared will 'reinforce their fear', but don't fret – calmly comforting your dog will help rather than hinder.

2

Desensitisation therapy

You can increase your dog's tolerance of scary noises by playing them firework and thunder sounds on a speaker. The beauty of this approach is that you can start at a 'safe' level, before very gradually increasing the intensity in a way your dog can deal with.

Pump up the bass
So you've been practising with scary sounds played through the speaker, starting quietly and getting louder over time. But what if your speaker isn't powerful enough to recreate the 'real' noise? You could borrow a powerful sound system with a sub-woofer. It'll be a banging party!

3

Bangs mean treats!

Once your dog is coping well, try sliding treats along the floor for them to chase and gobble after the practice sounds start playing (not before). The aim is for real loud noises to become signals for food and fun!

Take the show on the road
Random bangs on a walk can overly worry some dogs. To help your dog overcome this, use the same technique as before: pop a portable speaker in your backpack and play different noises as you wander along.

HOME ALONE

Many dogs get stressed when they're left alone, and their behaviour can be a big problem. By avoiding scary separations, while practising short, tolerable departures with consistent, reassuring routines, you can help your dog to relax while you're out.

SEPARATION IS HARD

Dogs are a social species – they normally like to be with their people or doggy friends. While many dogs tolerate being by themselves, some really don't feel good about time alone. They experience *anxiety* as a result of the isolation, and *frustration* at not being able to do anything about it. Their stressed emotional state and desire to get back to their family can mean they howl and bark, and attempt to scratch or chew through barriers such as the front door. Some dogs will pee or poo inside, or display other signs of anxiety (see pages 88–9). You can help to resolve this by teaching your dog how to cope with separation.

1
Safe room

Teach your dog that if you shut them in a specific room like the kitchen, you'll be back quickly – we're talking seconds not minutes here. Once your dog is handling those few seconds alone, you'll be able to slowly increase the duration.

Short and frequent
Keep the separations short, but frequent. If you're leaving your dog for only a few seconds at a time, you might open the door a crack, hand them a small food reward, and then shut the door again. Repeat ten times, then let your dog out and go on with the rest of your day.

Peek-a-boo!

See you soon Pickle!

2
Doggy monitor

Use a remote camera to watch your dog on your phone while the door is shut. If they are showing signs of stress (see pages 88–9), return to them, and decrease the length of time the door is shut next time. If your dog is coping, increase the duration by 10%. You need to push your dog's comfort zone a little, but don't stress them out.

Make it fun
Once your dog is able to cope alone for a full five minutes, begin to leave them with a stuffed Kong cone (see page 127) so they learn that *alone time means cone time!*

3
Go long

Practise easy departures five times a day, increasing the time your dog is in the safe room in small increments they can cope with. Add sounds that might occur during real departures, such as the front door opening and shutting. Because your dog is in the safe room and unable to see you, you won't need to practise other 'departure cues' like putting on shoes or a coat.

The real deal
Once they are happy in the safe room for 30 minutes, you're ready to try a real departure – but keep it short, and watch them on the doggy cam to check they're coping. Congratulations, you've helped your doggo conquer their fear!

LET'S TALK ABOUT GROOMING

Some dogs really don't want to be groomed. Brushing? Nail-clipping? It's time to find ways to teach your dog to enjoy those personal maintenance moments!

IT'S THAT TIME AGAIN...

Your dog's reluctance to be groomed is not because they prefer the grunge look, it's often that they feel nervous about being handled. Some dogs are naturally sensitive to being touched in some areas – and let's face it, having tangles brushed out or the experience of a nail being clipped too short isn't any fun, especially if they've been restrained in the past to get it done. It's a bit like us not being happy to be held down in a dentist's chair!

1

Easy and often

The best way to help your dog cope with handling is to avoid physically restraining them or pushing them past their comfort zone. Regularly have easy, fun grooming sessions where you *slightly* nudge their tolerance. Do this, and your dog's happiness with handling will slowly but surely improve.

OK, let's just use the soft brush today.

Respect their boundaries

If your dog mouths at your hand, bares their teeth, growls, snaps or struggles to move away, it's a sign they're not coping. Ease off the intensity, and keep it fun! You'll be surprised at the progress you make by respecting their boundaries.

Thanks for listening.

2

Distraction can backfire

It's tempting to try to distract your dog with food while you sneak in to deal with matted fur or clip a nail, but this actually teaches them to become wary and suspicious when food is on offer.

Time your treats

Teach your dog that touching means titbits. *While* the brush is running through their fur, or *while* you lift their ear, or *while* you're holding their paw to grind their nail, say 'Yes!' Stop the handling and reach for a super-treat.

3

Start fresh

If your dog's coat is matted and they don't cope well with grooming, this is clearly not a good place to begin teaching them that brushing is fun. Make a fresh start: ask your vet if they'd be happy to clip your dog's coat short under sedation, and then introduce daily, treat-filled grooming practice after that.

Nail grinder

If you clip a dog's nail too short, you can hit the 'quick', which is the live part of their nail. This really hurts, and can well and truly put dogs off nail-clippers! If that happens, switch to a nail grinder, which will carry no negative associations for them. It can also help reduce the chance of trimming too far in future.

UNDERSTANDING AGGRESSION

Seeing your dog behave aggressively can be confusing and worrying. Let's explore what's going on inside their head, and how you can help.

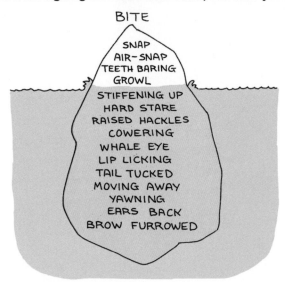

THE AGGRESSION ICEBERG

All dogs have the potential to behave aggressively when dealing with high-stake situations, like when they feel in danger, or if important stuff is up for grabs. While aggression can seem to come out of the blue, by the time you see snapping or biting, there have probably already been other, more elusive hints that your dog was uncomfortable. Your dog's behaviour is like an iceberg, with a lot going on unnoticed, below the surface.

Indications that our human radar might not pick up can include subtle signs of stress (see pages 88–9), or attempts to avoid the situation. Clearer warnings, like growling or teeth-baring, may occur if your dog's stress increases further. If things continue to escalate, you might see a brief freeze before your dog snaps or bites. Noticing the first below-the-surface signs is the key to understanding your dog, and helping them resolve situations without them pulling out the big guns.

1
Strong emotions

Aggression is often driven by strong emotions, such as fear, frustration and anger. Like us, a dog's emotions sometimes get the better of them, and they can lash out without thinking the situation through.

Cool down, then we'll talk.

Address emotion not behaviour
Rather than trying to deal with aggression while your dog is seeing red and not thinking straight, give them space, then, once they cool down, work to change the emotions that are driving their aggression.

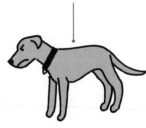

Reduce fear to reduce aggression
Help your dog learn to become more comfortable with things that scare them. Then, defensive aggression will become less likely.

2
Fear leading to aggression

One of the most common reasons a dog becomes aggressive is *fear*. If your dog feels they are in danger, aggression is a natural way for them to try to give themselves the space they need to feel safe.

3
Frustration ending in aggression

Some situations can be very frustrating for your dog. This frustration may occasionally bubble over into anger and an emotion-fuelled attempt to sort out the situation through aggression.

Grrr... My precious!

Removing resources
If you try to remove something your dog values highly – say food or a stolen glove – the spike in frustration your dog experiences might mean they lose their cool and lash out to keep the treasure! See pages 156–7 for ways to address this type of aggression.

STRANGER DANGER

The most common reason people bring their dog to see a professional behaviourist is that the dog has become aggressive towards unfamiliar dogs or people.

WHY DO DOGS REACT AGGRESSIVELY TO STRANGERS?

Canines who are the biggest softies at home with their family can turn into lunging, growling, barking, biting, stress-monsters when near unfamiliar dogs or strangers. In most cases, this aggressive front is actually driven by fear and a desire to move the 'dangerous' strangers away.

Controlling your dog in these situations is challenging, as they're often in the fight-or-flight state, and not thinking straight (see page 142). However, by slowly but surely teaching your dog that new individuals are safe, and teaching them how you want them to behave if they are nervous, you can start to change your reactive Rover into a happy hound.

1

Safety

If your dog is reactive near strangers, first and foremost keep everybody safe. Ensuring your dog has the space they need is very important. Also, your dog can wear a muzzle to reduce the risk that they will cause injury if they get stressed and bite (see pages 50–51).

Management tools
Sometimes 'normal' collars or back-attaching harnesses (see page 49) can mean it is difficult to control your dog if they become stressed and reactive. Consider a headcollar or chest-attaching harness, which will allow you to manage their behaviour more effectively.

New dogs are fun!

2

Safe social sessions

By spending time near unfamiliar dogs or people, but at a distance your dog can cope with, your dog will slowly start to feel safer around strangers. They'll be less likely to get stressed and 'shouty' about their desire for space.

Let's get to know each other
Once your dog is coping with being near strangers, try building on this progress. If they relax enough to take a treat dropped on the ground from a stranger, or to start a bout of play with a new dog, this can help your dog feel even more confident.

3

An alternative behaviour...

Train your dog how to behave when they're feeling on edge about a stranger. Simple works best – if your dog voluntarily looks up at you when they're worried about someone, say an encouraging 'Yes!' and then reach for a super-treat.

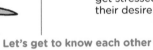

...And a new emotion
Not only will rewarding eye-contact with a treat teach your dog how to behave, it will also help improve the emotion driving their reactivity. Strangers will predict a super-treat from you ('Yay! Food!'), rather than a risk to life and limb ('Eek! Danger!').

Strangers mean treats.

DOGS WHO BITE PEOPLE THEY LOVE

When a dog bites someone they love, it can feel as if they have breached our trust. By understanding what is behind your dog's aggression, you'll understand it's not personal, and you'll be able to help your dog by building a more harmonious relationship with them.

IS YOUR DOG FEELING FRUSTRATED?

When dogs behave aggressively towards their family, it's often a result of frustration getting the better of them. Either they anticipate they are going to lose something valuable, something is happening they really don't like, or they are being stopped from doing something important to them. This frustration bubbles over into them losing their cool and resorting to aggression to control the situation.

Rather than viewing this as an attempt to 'dominate' you, think of it as a toddler temper tantrum with teeth!

1

Don't fight fire with fire

Punishing your dog when they are seeing red can fuel the emotions driving their behaviour, increasing the aggression both in the moment, and in the long term.

Avoid triggers

If your dog loses their cool and behaves aggressively, give them some space and let the moment pass. Try to set up your dog's life to reduce these flash-points in the future.

Let's give you space to enjoy your chew outside, Max.

Sit!

Yay, a request!

2

Work on the foundations

Make sure your dog is in the habit of responding to your requests, and that good things happen when they do (see pages 40–41 and 54–5). By developing your leadership role, they will be more likely to look to you for direction in challenging situations.

Positive vibes

Working on the foundations of your relationship will reduce emotions, such as frustration and fear, that might be driving your dog's aggression.

3

Change their expectations

Focus on training in situations your dog finds stressful. Rather than trying to curb aggression in the moment by 'teaching them who's boss', improve their expectations and emotions in these situations through positive and proactive training.*

* If your dog is behaving aggressively, seek the advice of an accredited dog behaviourist to ensure you're doing the best for your dog and to reduce the risk of being bitten.

Drop Teddy, get treat, get Teddy back.

Swap and return

If you have a dog who behaves aggressively around resources, teach them that if they voluntarily give something up, you'll often surprise them with a super-treat, *and then give the item back.* Sure, you'll need to permanently confiscate some items (Grandad's glasses), but you should practise regularly with 'safe' items. For your dog, 'drop' will start to mean 'there's something to gain', rather than 'they're going to take it away'. If your dog feels less frustrated and stressed around resources, they'll be less aggressive.

TERRITORIAL TENSION

Barking at the postman is what being a dog is all about, but some dogs take their role as territorial defenders a bit too seriously!

Step away from the perimeter!

WHY DO DOGS BEHAVE TERRITORIALLY?

Do you have a dog who thinks the doorbell is a signal for imminent household invasion? Do other dogs passing the front window trigger a frenzy of barking?

Dogs can be formidable burglar alarms, but sometimes their commitment to the job can be worrying, especially if their bark is followed by a bite.

Three things often drive this territorial behaviour:

- an *instinctual* urge to defend their patch

- *increased confidence* owing to being in their familiar environment

- a *history* of successfully keeping 'intruders' at bay – it's a self-rewarding thrill!

1

What a dog can't see...

Every time your dog barks at something passing, their territorial behaviour is rewarded, and becomes a little more ingrained. Stand your dog down from their territorial responsibilities by blocking their ability to see 'intruders'.

Glass frosting

Often the street-facing windows of a house are key territorial patrol points. By putting frosting film on the bottom sections of the windows, light can still enter your home, but you'll reduce your dog's barking, stop the self-reinforcement of their territorial defence, and make your dog's life less stressful – as well as your own.

Go to my place, get treat!

DING DONG

2

Doorbell training

For many dogs the sound of the doorbell triggers a surge of adrenaline, and intense territorial behaviour like barking that's very hard to interrupt. To change both their emotional and behavioural response to the doorbell, practise a fun routine where every time they hear the bell, they will earn a treat if they move to their bed.

Start fresh

The easiest way to begin doorbell training is to start fresh with an electronic bell that has two buttons – one for your pocket, and one for the door. Ten times a day push the button in your pocket, and reward your dog for going to their special place. With enough practice, they'll head straight there when visitors ring the same bell from outside.

3

Keep safe

Many dogs can put up a ferocious front, but turn into friendly teddy bears once they actually meet visitors. However, some do mean business, and can bite. Keep everyone safe by moving your dog to another room before opening the door. Ask your visitors to come in and sit down, then bring your dog in on a lead.* This way everyone has a chance to get to know each other away from the chaos and confrontation at the front door.

Nice to meet you

If your visitors give your dog space, remain seated, and throw the occasional titbit, your dog will learn to love them!

I love this visitor.

* With a muzzle if necessary to keep your visitors 100% safe (see pages 50–51).

TEN GOLDEN RULES FOR A HAPPY LIFE WITH YOUR DOG

1 **Meet the parents.**

Pick a puppy whose parents are healthy, friendly and relaxed, and ensure they are raised in the breeder's home rather than an outside building. This will give your puppy the best chance of coping with and enjoying life's future challenges (pages 26–7).

2 **100 people, 100 dogs, 100 places.**

Provide your puppy with many different disease-safe experiences before they are 12 weeks old. This will set them up to become tolerant, confident, sociable adult dogs (pages 30–31).

3 **Learn your dog's language.**

By learning the subtleties of dog communication, you'll better understand your dog's emotions and needs (pages 80–89).

4 **Train desirable behaviour (rather than stopping unwanted behaviour).**

Teach your dog how you want them to behave, and make it pay off for them – you'll reduce unwanted behaviour and your dog will be happier (pages 54–5).

5 **Reward, but don't bribe.**

It's amazing what the occasional reward for good behaviour can achieve, but remember: rather than luring your dog with a bribe *to do something*, surprise them with a reward *after they listen* (pages 58–61)!

6 **Ditch dominance as an explanation for your dog's behaviour.**

Don't let the dominance myth get in the way of a fulfilling relationship with your pooch. Be a good parent rather than worrying about 'pack leadership' (pages 38-9).

7 **Teach your dog to 'learn to earn'.**

Provide access to things your dog desires after they respond to a simple request. This will establish a relationship where they look to you for direction in order to succeed (pages 40-41).

8 **An ounce of prevention is better than a pound of cure.**

Prioritise your dog's health to help them achieve a long and happy life (pages 96-111).

9 **Brain games enrich your dog's life.**

Do away with the food bowl and use your dog's daily food ration to create fun activities for them every day (pages 126-7).

10 **Play, play, play!**

Play is such fun for your dog, and it has *many other* benefits – including cementing a close relationship between you (pages 44-5).

BLOOMSBURY PUBLISHING
Bloomsbury Publishing Plc
50 Bedford Square, London, WC1B 3DP, UK
29 Earlsfort Terrace, Dublin 2, Ireland

BLOOMSBURY, BLOOMSBURY PUBLISHING and the Diana logo are trademarks of
Bloomsbury Publishing Plc

First published in Great Britain 2021

The information contained in this book is provided by way of general guidance in relation to the specific subject matters addressed herein, but it is not a substitute for specialist veterinary, behaviour or training advice. It should not be relied on for medical, healthcare, pharmaceutical, training, management, safety or other professional advice on specific animal behaviour needs. This book is sold with the understanding that the author and publisher are not engaged in rendering medical, health, behaviour, training or any other kind of personal or professional services. The reader should consult a competent veterinary health professional or clinical dog behaviourist before adopting any of the suggestions in this book or drawing inferences from it.

The author and publisher specifically disclaim, as far as the law allows, any responsibility from any liability, loss or risk (personal or otherwise) which is incurred as a consequence, directly or indirectly, of the use and applications of any of the contents of this book

A catalogue record for this book is available from the British Library

Library of Congress Cataloguing-in-Publication data has been applied for

ISBN: HB: 978-1-5266-3995-0; eBook: 978-1-5266-3996-7

2 4 6 8 10 9 7 5 3 1

Commissioning Editor: Xa Shaw Stewart
Project Editor: Jude Barratt
Design Layout: Phillip Beresford
Illustrator: Rupert Fawcett

Printed and bound in China by C&C Offset Printing Co, Ltd

Bloomsbury Publishing Plc makes every effort to ensure that the papers used in the manufacture of our books are natural, recyclable products made from wood grown in well-managed forests. Our manufacturing processes conform to the environmental regulations of the country of origin

To find out more about our authors and books visit www.bloomsbury.com
and sign up for our newsletters

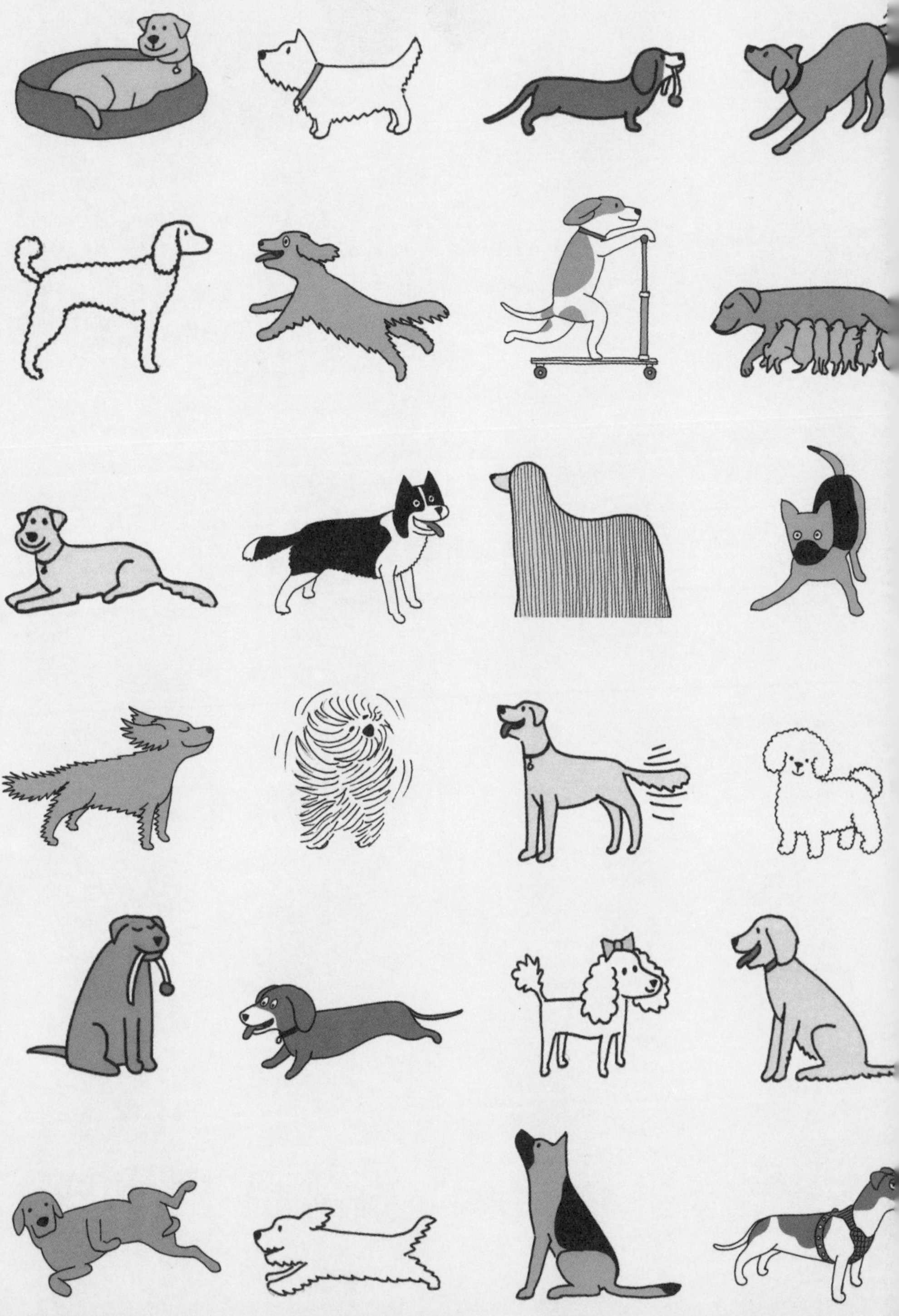